PRESCHOOL WORKBOOK

EARLY LEARNING ACTIVITIES FOR READING READINESS, NUMBERS, HANDWRITING, AND MORE

ZONDERKIDZ

The Beginner's Bible Preschool Workbook
Copyright © 2021 by Zondervan
Illustrations © 2021 by Zondervan

Requests for information should be addressed to:
Zonderkidz, 3900 *Sparks Dr. SE, Grand Rapids, Michigan 49546*

ISBN: 9780310751670
ISBN: 9781404118928 (Custom)

Editor: Mary Hassinger
Interior design: Denise Froehlich

Printed in Bosnia and Herzegovina

23 24 25 26 27 /GPS/ 7 6 5 4 3 2

AGES 3 - 5

Table of Contents

My name is _____.

I am _____ years old.

I am **ready** to learn!

Noah's Ark

Noah built an ark. Trace the lines.

Trace the lines top to bottom.

Trace lines left to right, going down.

Trace lines left to right, going up.

Trace arcs up to down.

Promised Land Pathway

Follow the lines. Help God's people find the promised land.

Saul Gets a Crown

God chose Saul to be the king.
Trace the shapes. Design and color a crown for Saul.

God Is Good

The Lord is my shepherd. God's goodness and love will follow me all the days of my life. Help the sheep find the shepherd.

Home Sweet Home

The son wanted to go home.
Help him find his way home.

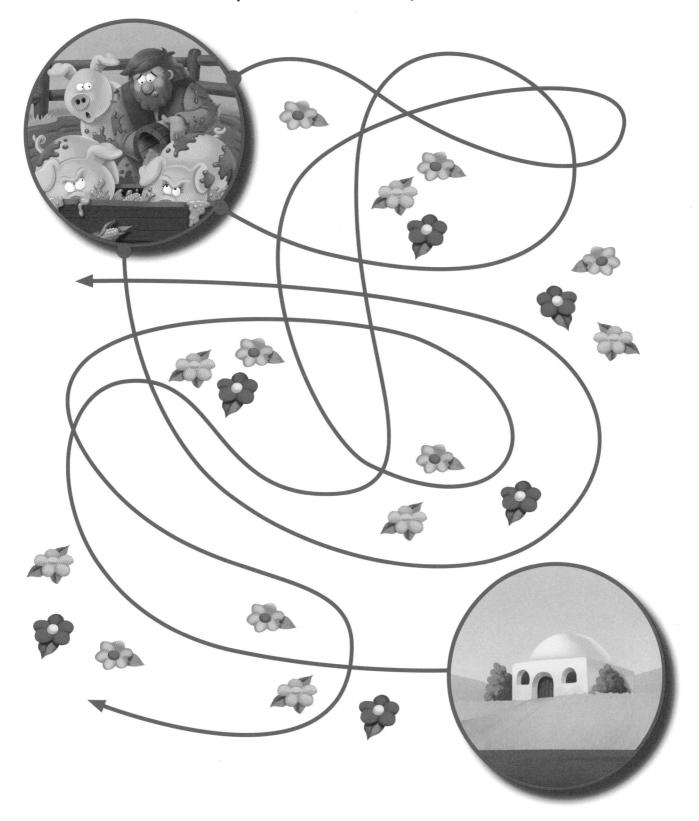

Circle Around

There is no beginning and no end to God's love. There is no beginning and end to a circle. Trace the circles.

Left to Right

God said the snake would crawl on its belly.
Trace the long snake, left to right.

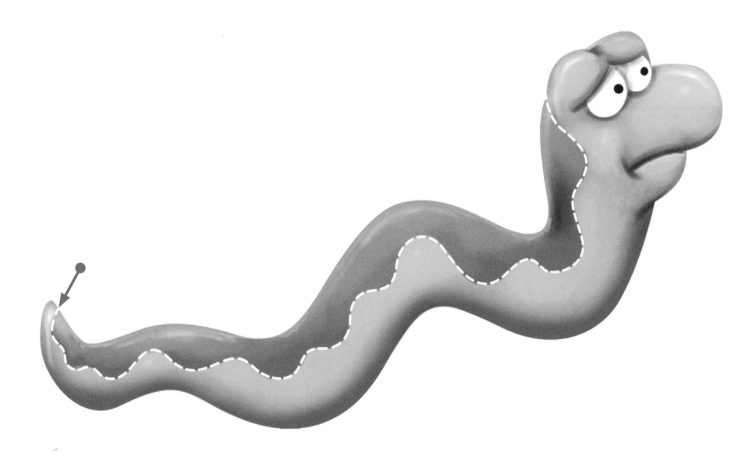

Waves Apart

The Lord pushed back the sea to make a path.
Trace the waves left to right.

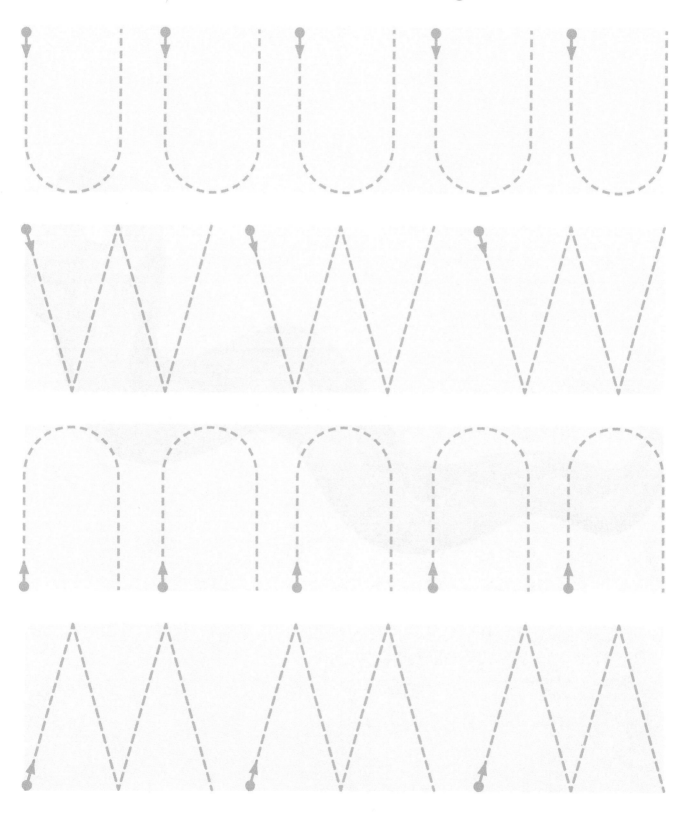

Where Is the Baby?

The angels said, "Go see the baby King!" Which path did the shepherds take to find baby Jesus? Trace the path.

Copy Me

Trace the lines with a pencil. Copy the lines yourself.

Copy Me Too

Trace the lines with a pencil. Copy the lines yourself.

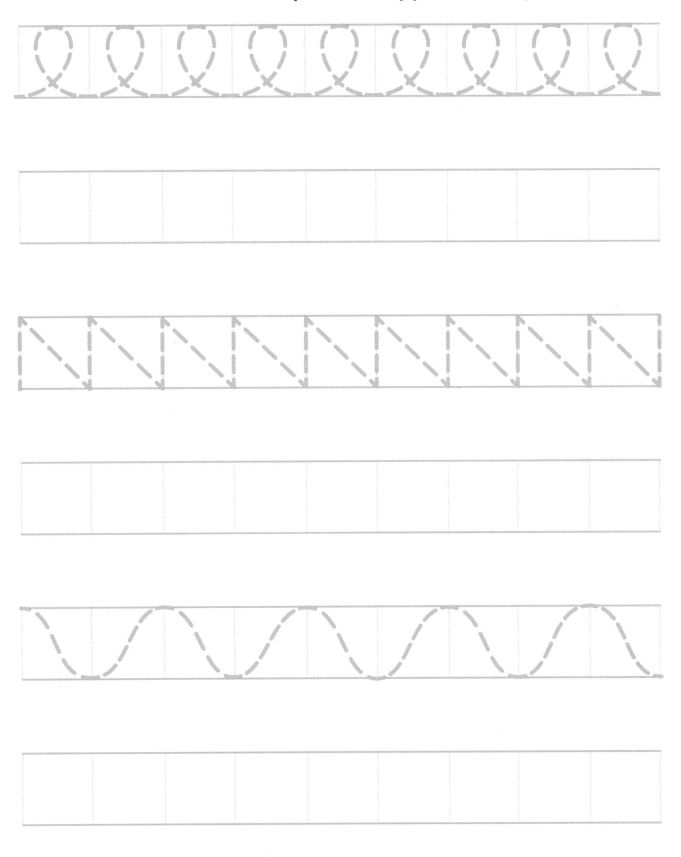

Trace Me!

Trace the lines. Help the animals find their friends.

Tracing Lines

Trace the lines from the dots to the animals.

Trace the Letters

Trace the uppercase and lowercase letters.

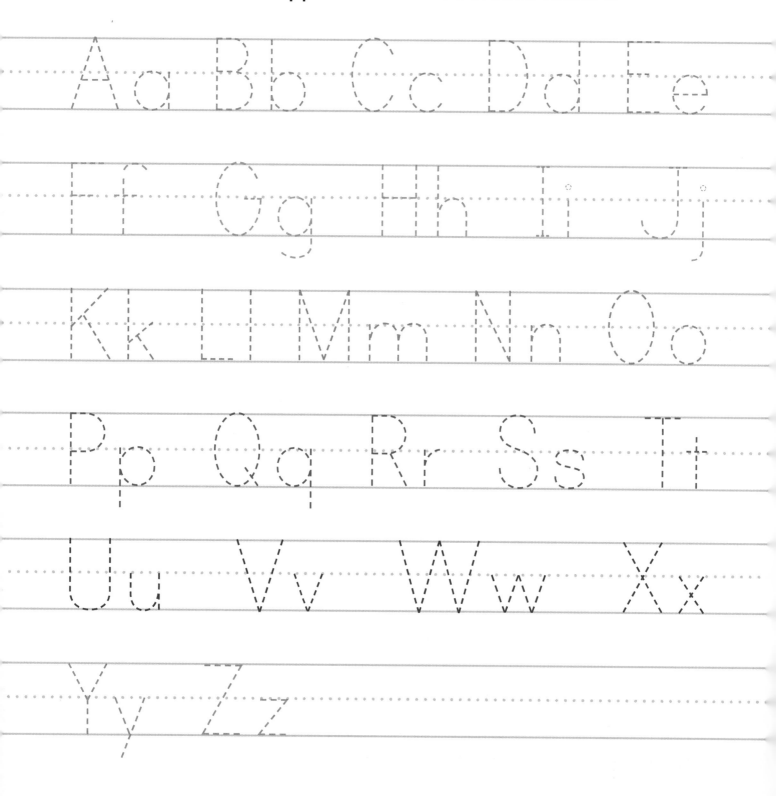

Trace Again

Trace the uppercase and lowercase letters.

Aa Bb Cc Dd Ee

Ff Gg Hh Ii Jj

Kk Ll Mm Nn Oo

Pp Qq Rr Ss Tt

Uu Vv Ww Xx

Yy Zz

Learn the Letter Aa

Trace the letter Aa. Then write Aa on your own. Fill the lines.

Now circle the **Aa** in each word.

Adam

ark

arrow

angel

Learn the Letter Bb

Trace the letter Bb. Then write Bb on your own. Fill the lines.

Now circle the **Bb** in each word.

bread   **boat**

baby   **bird**

Learn the Letter Cc

Trace the letter Cc. Then write Cc on your own. Fill the lines.

Now circle the Cc in each word.

crab

cross

corn

cat

Learn the Letter Dd

Trace the letter Dd. Then write Dd on your own. Fill the lines.

D D D

d d d

Now circle the Dd in each word.

David

dove

dog

donkey

Learn the Letter Ee

Trace the letter Ee. Then write Ee on your own. Fill the lines.

E E E E

e e e

Now circle the Ee in each word.

elephant

eyes

eat

Eve

Learn the Letter Ff

Trace the letter Ff. Then write Ff on your own. Fill the lines.

F F F

f f f

Now circle the **Ff** in each word.

flowers

frog

fish

fruit

Learn the Letter Gg

Trace the letter Gg. Then write Gg on your own. Fill the lines.

G G G

g g g

Now circle the Gg in each word.

gifts

garden

Goliath

girl

Learn the Letter Hh

Trace the letter Hh. Then write Hh on your own. Fill the lines.

H H H

h h h

Now circle the Hh in each word.

honey

hat

house

hug

Learn the Letter Ii

Trace the letter Ii. Then write Ii on your own. Fill the lines.

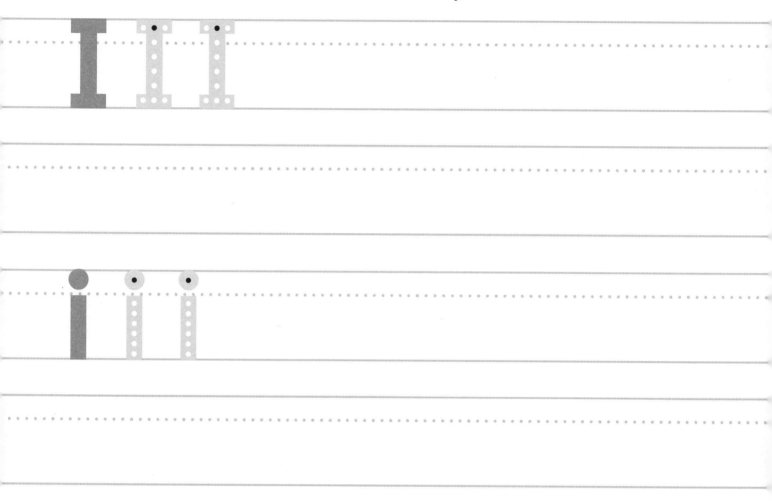

Now circle the Ii in each word.

inn

infant

Isaac

Learn the Letter Jj

Trace the letter Jj. Then write Jj on your own. Fill the lines.

Now circle the Jj in each word.

Jesus

jars

jewel

Jonah

Learn the Letter Kk

Trace the letter Kk. Then write Kk on your own. Fill the lines.

K K K

k k k

Now circle the Kk in each word.

kneel

king

keys

Learn the Letter Ll

Trace the letter Ll. Then write Ll on your own. Fill the lines.

Now circle the Ll in each word.

lamp

lamb

lion

leaf

Learn the Letter Mm

Trace the letter Mm. Then write Mm on your own. Fill the lines.

M M M

m m m

Now circle the Mm in each word.

man

moon

manger

money

Learn the Letter Nn

Trace the letter Nn. Then write Nn on your own. Fill the lines.

NNN

nnn

Now circle the Nn in each word.

night

Noah

net

Learn the Letter Oo

Trace the letter Oo. Then write Oo on your own. Fill the lines.

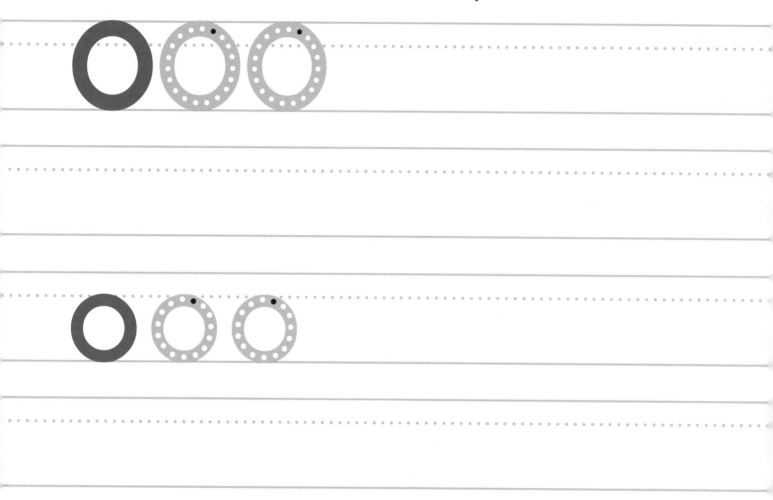

Now circle the Oo in each word.

old

oil

octopus

offering

Learn the Letter Pp

Trace the letter Pp. Then write Pp on your own. Fill the lines.

P P P P

p p p p

Now circle the Pp in each word.

plate

pyramid

pray

pigs

Learn the Letter Qq

Trace the letter Qq. Then write Qq on your own. Fill the lines.

Q Q Q

q q q

Now circle the Qq in each word.

queen

quill

question

quail

Learn the Letter Rr

Trace the letter Rr. Then write Rr on your own. Fill the lines.

Now circle the Rr in each word.

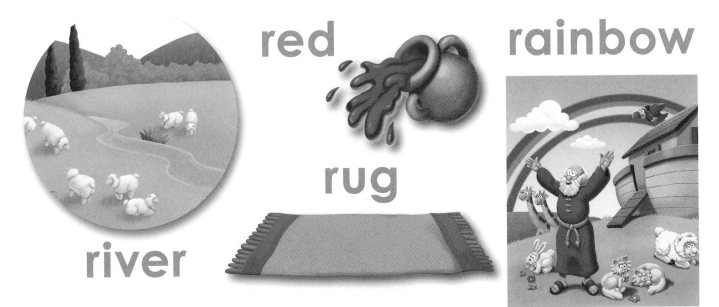

river

red

rug

rainbow

Learn the Letter Ss

Trace the letter Ss. Then write Ss on your own. Fill the lines.

S S S

s s s

Now circle the Ss in each word.

sheep

sun

star

snake

Learn the Letter Tt

Trace the letter Tt. Then write Tt on your own. Fill the lines.

Now circle the Tt in each word.

tear

tree

table

tomb

Learn the Letter Uu

Trace the letter Uu. Then write Uu on your own. Fill the lines.

U U U

U U U

Now circle the Uu in each word.

uncle

under

upset

Learn the Letter Vv

Trace the letter Vv. Then write Vv on your own. Fill the lines.

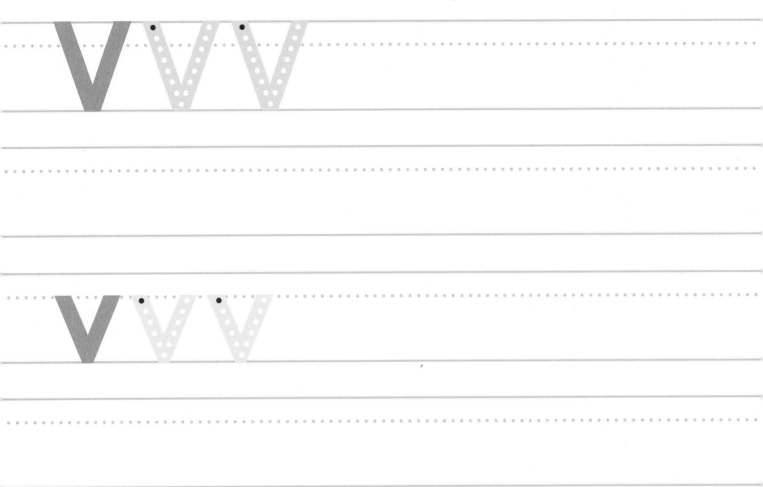

Now circle the Vv in each word.

vine

vase

visitors

Learn the Letters Ww and Xx

Trace the letters Ww and Xx. Then write Ww and xx on your own. Fill the lines.

Now circle the Ww and Xx in each word.

water

window

ox

extra

Learn the Letters Yy and Zz

Trace the letters Yy and Zz. Then write Yy and Zz on your own. Fill the lines.

Y Y Y

y y y

Z Z Z

Z Z Z

Now circle the Yy and Zz in each word.

yell

yes

Zacchaeus

zebra

Color the Letter Aa

Find and color uppercase A **red**. Find and color the lowercase a **yellow**.

Color the Letter Bb

Find and color the uppercase B blue. Find
and color the lowercase b orange.

Color the Letter Cc

Find and color the uppercase C **brown**.
Find and color the lowercase c **pink**.

Color the Letter Dd

Find and color the uppercase D green. Find and color the lowercase d blue.

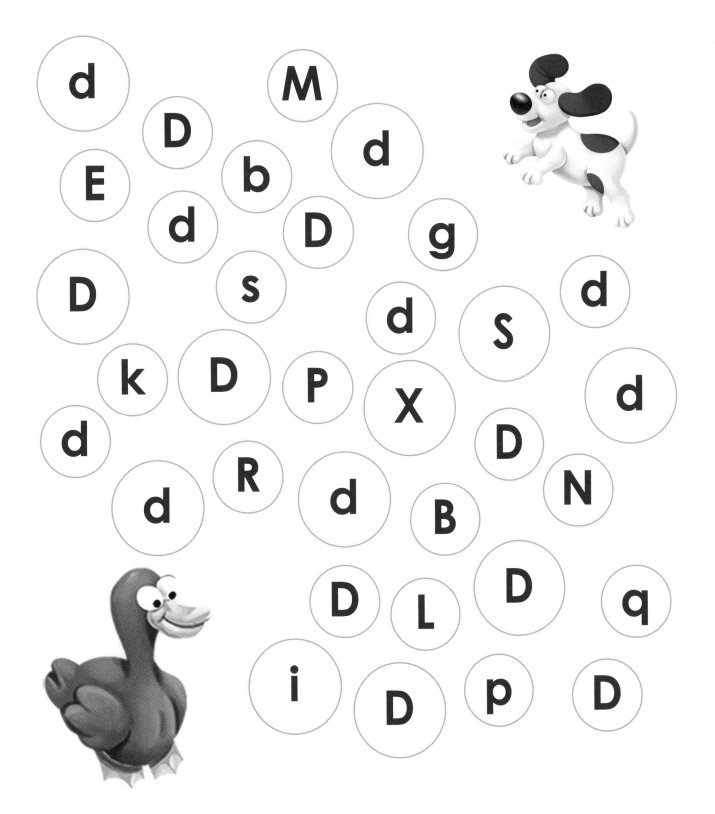

Color the Letter Ee

Find and color the uppercase E **purple**.
Find and color the lowercase e **red**.

Color the Letter Ff

Find and color the uppercase F yellow. Find and color the lowercase f orange.

Color the Letter Gg

Find and color the uppercase G green. Find and color the lowercase g blue.

Color the Letter Hh

Find and color the uppercase H **purple**. Find and color the lowercase h orange.

Color the Letter Ii

Find and color the uppercase I **red**. Find
and color the lowercase i **yellow**.

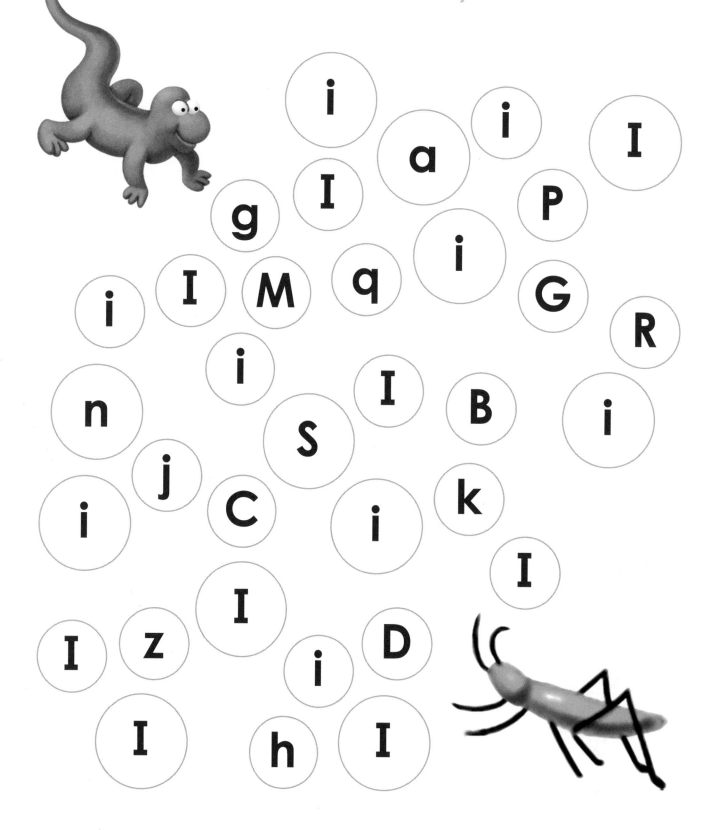

Color the Letter Jj

Find and color the uppercase J **brown**. Find and color the lowercase j **pink**.

jellyfish

Color the Letter Kk

Find and color the uppercase K blue. Find and color the lowercase k orange.

K g k q K

K z j M

k k K F

t k

H K K k L L A K

k T

k k k

K s e K w k

K

k D

Color the Letter Ll

Find and color the uppercase L **yellow**. Find and color the lowercase l **purple**.

Color the Letter Mm

Find and color the uppercase M green. Find
and color the lowercase m blue.

Color the Letter Nn

Find and color the uppercase N **brown**. Find and color the lowercase n **pink**.

Noah

Color the Letter Oo

Find and color the uppercase O **red**. Find and color the lowercase o **blue**.

Color the Letter Pp

Find and color the uppercase P purple. Find and color the lowercase p yellow.

Color the Letter Qq

Find and color the uppercase Q green. Find and color the lowercase q orange.

squirrel

Color the Letter Rr

Find and color the uppercase R blue. Find
and color the lowercase r pink.

Y
r Q
Y R r
r c V
r R r R
R R r r K p
w L r A r
R r R R E R
b r r H
s e
Z d
R R

Color the Letter Ss

Find and color the uppercase S **yellow**. Find and color the lowercase s **purple**.

Color the Letter Tt

Find and color the uppercase T green. Find
and color the lowercase t blue.

Color the Letter Uu

Find and color the uppercase U **blue**. Find and color the lowercase u **purple**.

sea <u>u</u>rchin

Color the Letter Vv

Find and color the uppercase V **brown**. Find
and color the lowercase v **pink**.

E V v A
S V
v
K u d v p
V e v V Z
e
v c H v
b v V
Y V V w
L v
V V
Q V
v

beaver

Color the Letter Ww

Find and color the uppercase W orange.
Find and color the lowercase w green.

Color the Letter Xx

Find and color the uppercase X **red**. Find and color the lowercase x **yellow**.

X x i E e X x b W x J X X G x q x X S g x k X B X N a X R X x X v

Color the Letter Yy

Find and color the uppercase Y **purple**.
Find and color the lowercase y **blue**.

donkey

Color the Letter Zz

Find and color the uppercase Z **pink**. Find and color the lowercase z **orange**.

zebra

Write It Out—Aa

Name the pictures. Trace and write A. Trace and write a.

angel

ark

apple

A A

a a

Trace the words. Then write the words.

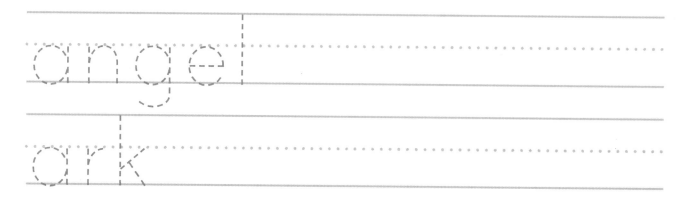

angel

ark

Write It Out—Bb

Name the pictures. Trace and write **B**. Trace and write **b**.

bird

butterfly

bunny

Trace the words. Then write the words.

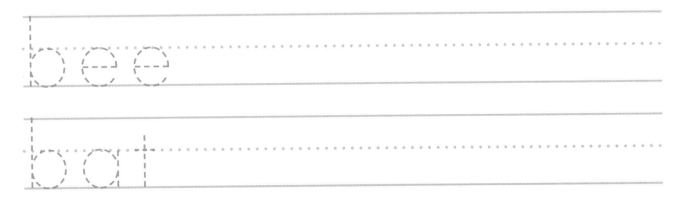

bee

bat

Write It Out—Cc

Name the pictures. Trace and write C. Trace and write c.

crab

cow

cat

C C

c c

Trace the words. Then write the words.

cat

cow

Write It Out—Dd

Name the pictures. Trace and write D. Trace and write d.

dance

duck

dove

Trace the words. Then write the words.

Write It Out—Ee

Name the pictures. Trace and write **E**. Trace and write **e**.

elephant

Eve

egg

E E

e e

Trace the words. Then write the words.

egg

eel

Write It Out—Ff

Name the pictures. Trace and write F. Trace and write f.

fish

flowers

frog

Trace the words. Then write the words.

fan

fish

Write It Out—Gg

Name the pictures. Trace and write **G**. Trace and write **g**.

gifts

grasshopper

giant

G G

g g

Trace the words. Then write the words.

God

girl

Write It Out—Hh

Name the pictures. Trace and write H. Trace and write h.

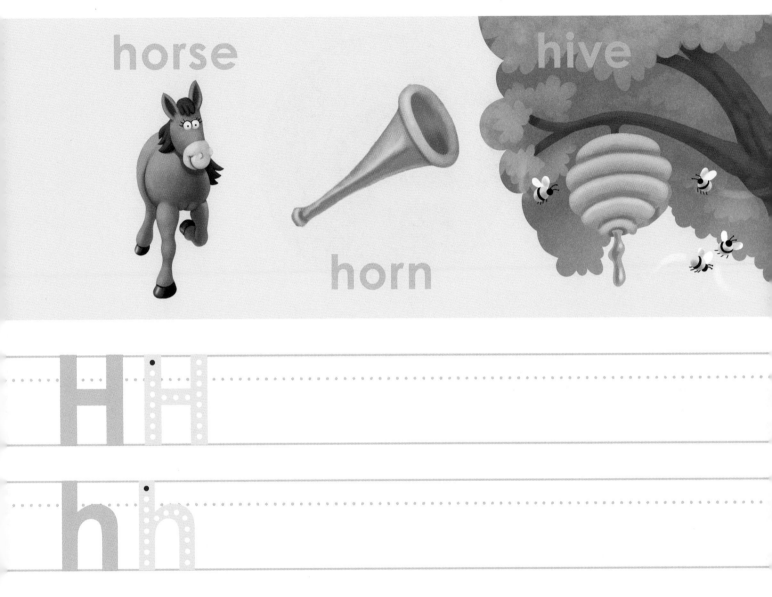

horse

hive

horn

Trace the words. Then write the words.

Write It Out—Ii

Name the pictures. Trace and write I. Trace and write i.

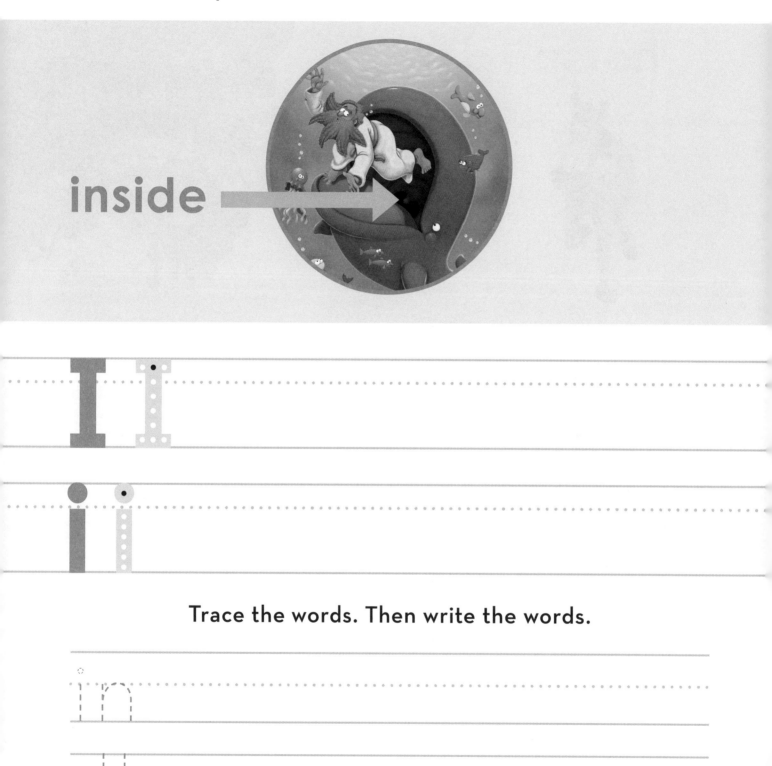

inside

Trace the words. Then write the words.

Write It Out—Jj

Name the pictures. Trace and write J. Trace and write j.

jar

Jesus

jug

J J

j j

Trace the words. Then write the words.

jet

jar

Write It Out—Kk

Name the pictures. Trace and write **K**. Trace and write **k**.

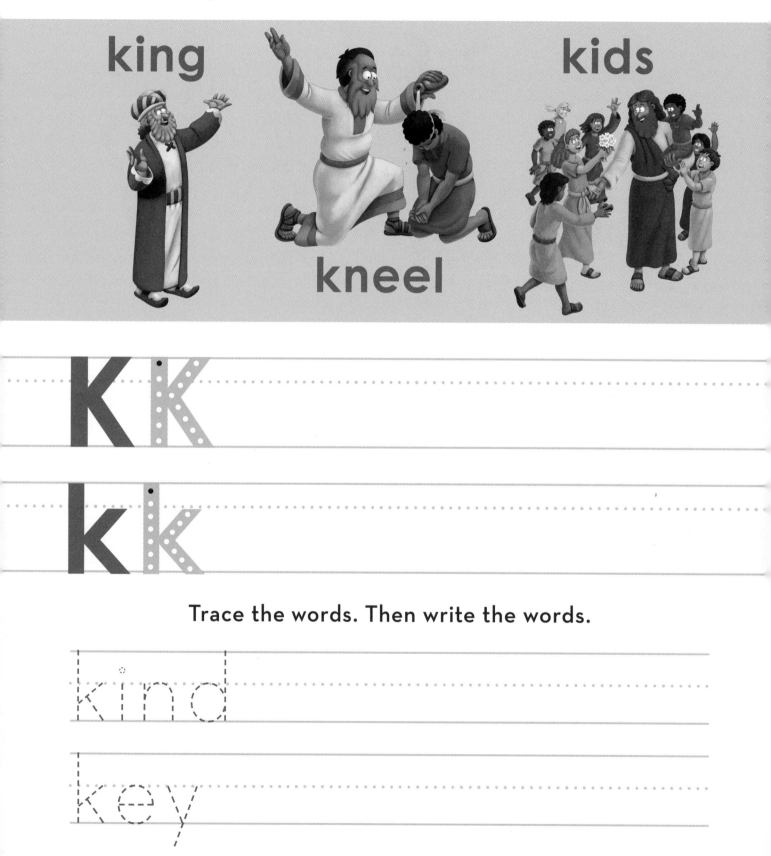

king

kneel

kids

K K

k k

Trace the words. Then write the words.

kind

key

Write It Out—Ll

Name the pictures. Trace and write L. Trace and write l.

lizard

lamp

legs

Trace the words. Then write the words.

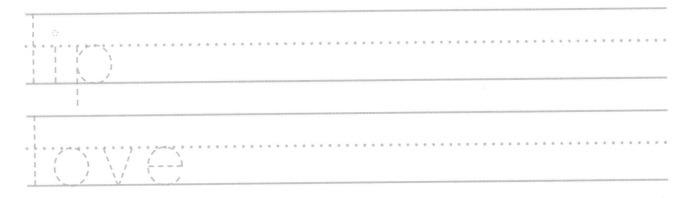

lip

love

Write It Out—Mm

Name the pictures. Trace and write M. Trace and write m.

mice

mad

monkey

M M

m m

Trace the words. Then write the words.

man

mop

Write It Out—Nn

Name the pictures. Trace and write **N**. Trace and write **n**.

Trace the words. Then write the words.

no

net

Write It Out—Oo

Name the pictures. Trace and write O. Trace and write o.

ox

oil

owl

Trace the words. Then write the words.

ox

owl

Write It Out—Pp

Name the pictures. Trace and write P. Trace and write p.

plant

push

pail

P P

p p

Trace the words. Then write the words.

pup

pig

Write It Out—Qq

Name the pictures. Trace and write Q. Trace and write q.

queen

quill

quack

Q Q

q q

Trace the words. Then write the words.

queen

quack

Write It Out—Rr

Name the pictures. Trace and write **R**. Trace and write **r**.

run

road

read

R R R

r r

Trace the words. Then write the words.

run

ring

Write It Out—Ss

Name the pictures. Trace and write **S**. Trace and write **s**.

sweep

sleep

squirrel

Trace the words. Then write the words.

sun

sad

Write It Out—Tt

Name the pictures. Trace and write T. Trace and write t.

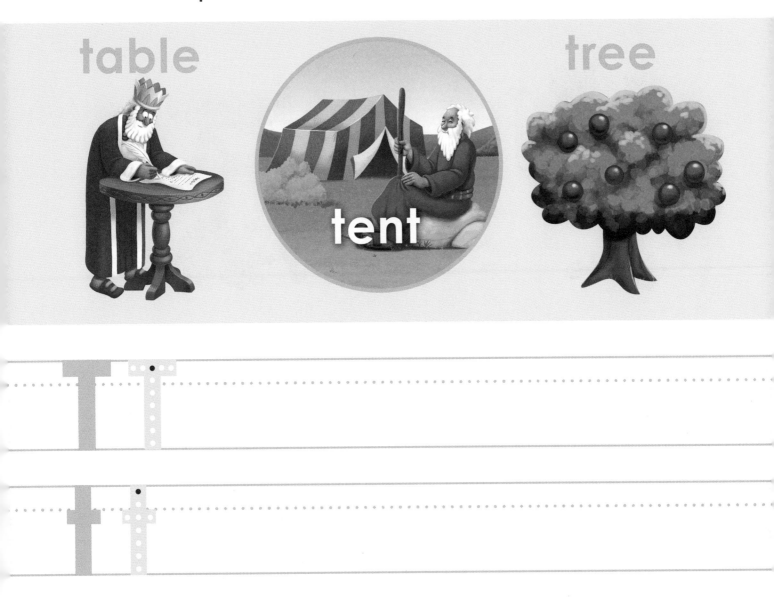

table

tent

tree

Trace the words. Then write the words.

tree

tall

Write It Out—Uu

Name the pictures. Trace and write **U**. Trace and write **u**.

↑ up

under →

U U U

U U U

Trace the words. Then write the words.

up

us

Write It Out—Vv

Name the pictures. Trace and write V. Trace and write v.

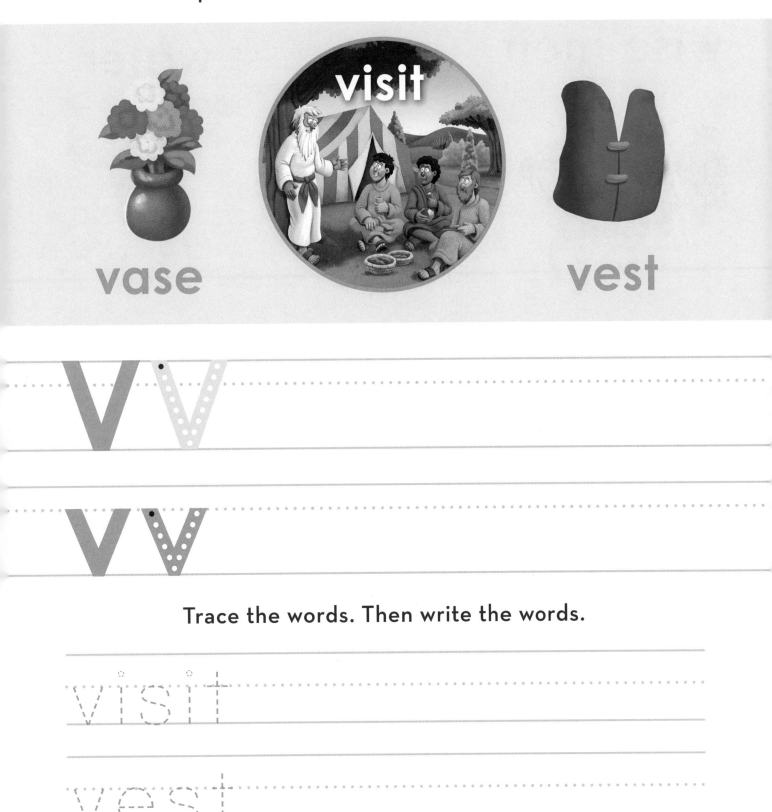

vase

visit

vest

V V

v v

Trace the words. Then write the words.

visit

vest

Write It Out—Ww

Name the pictures. Trace and write W. Trace and write w.

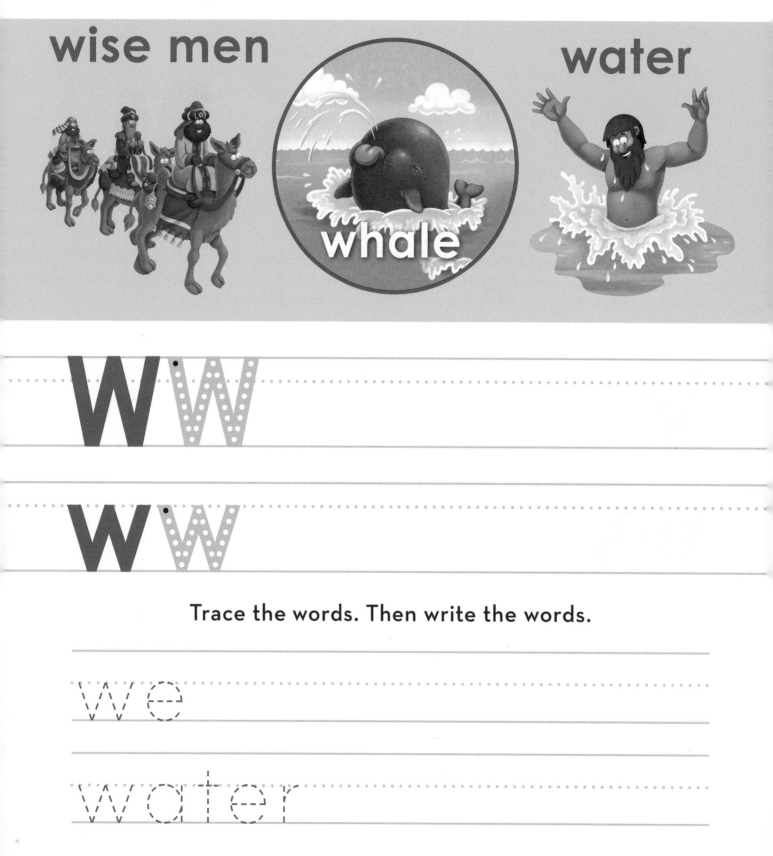

wise men

whale

water

W W

w w

Trace the words. Then write the words.

we

water

Write It Out—Xx

Name the pictures. Trace and write X. Trace and write x.

X X

X X

Trace the words. Then write the words.

ox

tox

Write It Out—Yy

Name the pictures. Trace and write Y. Trace and write y.

← yellow

yell

Y Y

y y

Trace the words. Then write the words.

yak

yam

Write It Out—Zz

Name the pictures. Trace and write Z. Trace and write z.

buzz

Zacchaeus

Zz

Zz

Trace the words. Then write the words.

zero

zip

In the Beginning

Connect the picture with its beginning sound. One is done for you.

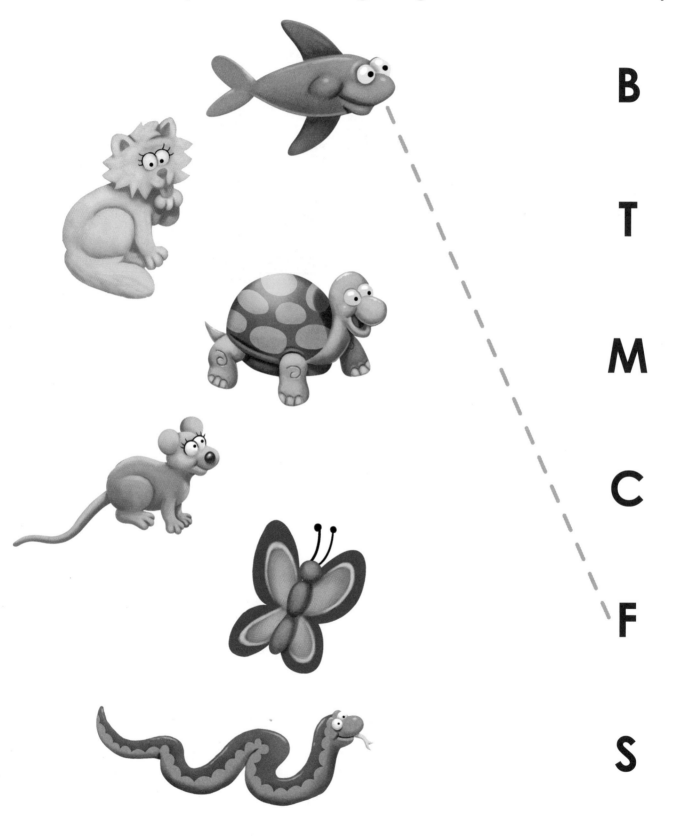

B

T

M

C

F

S

It Starts Here

Connect the picture with its beginning sound. One is done for you.

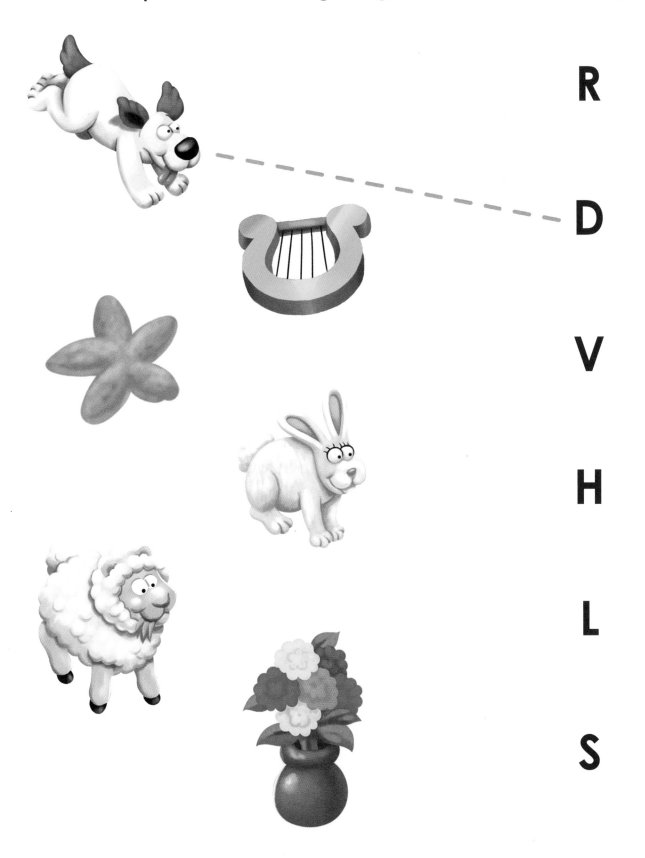

R

D

V

H

L

S

Sounds the Same—B

Bee, butterfly, and bird start with **B**. Write **Bb**.

butterfly

bee

bird

Now circle all the Bbs you see.

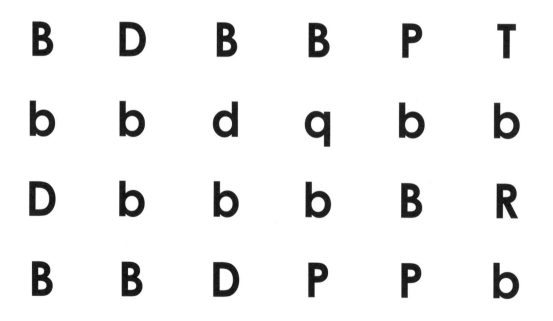

B	D	B	B	P	T
b	b	d	q	b	b
D	b	b	b	B	R
B	B	D	P	P	b

Sounds the Same—C

Cat, corn, and cup start with C. Write Cc.

cat

corn

cup

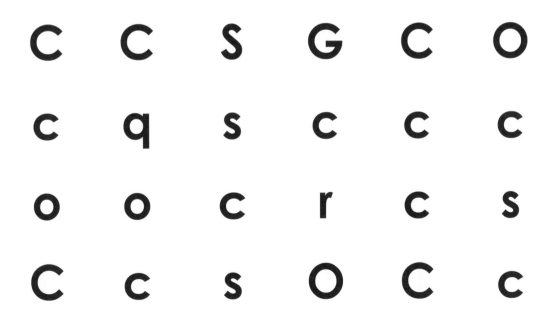

Now circle all the Ccs you see.

C   C   S   G   C   O

c   q   s   c   c   c

o   o   c   r   c   s

C   c   s   O   C   c

Sounds the Same—F

Fish, flower, and food start with F. Write Ff.

fish

flowers

food

Ff

Now circle all the Ffs you see.

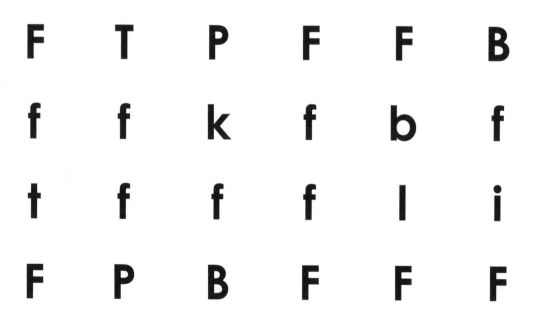

F	T	P	F	F	B
f	f	k	f	b	f
t	f	f	f	l	i
F	P	B	F	F	F

Sounds the Same—T

Tree, tools, and twigs start with T. Write Tt.

tree

tools

twigs

Now circle all the Tts you see.

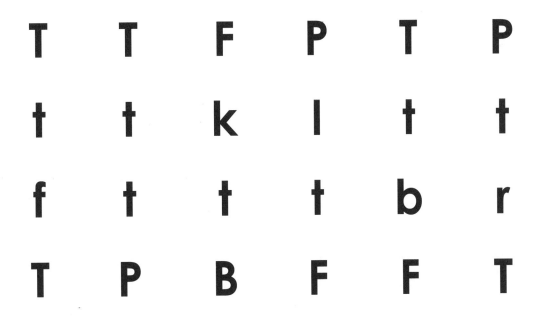

T   T   F   P   T   P

t   t   k   l   t   t

f   t   t   t   b   r

T   P   B   F   F   T

Sounds the Same—S

Saw, sail, and sad start with S. Write Ss.

saw

sail

sad

Ss

Now circle all the **Sss** you see.

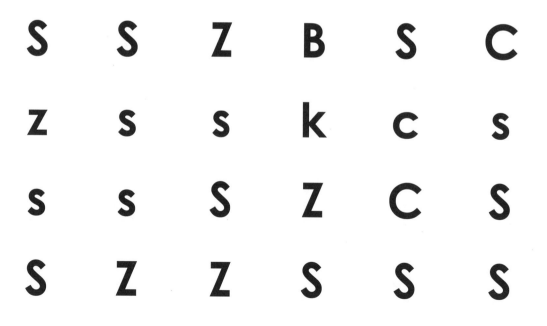

S	S	Z	B	S	C
z	s	s	k	c	s
s	s	S	Z	C	S
S	Z	Z	S	S	S

I Know the Sound

Say the name of the picture. Circle the letter that starts the picture name. Write the letter three times on the line.

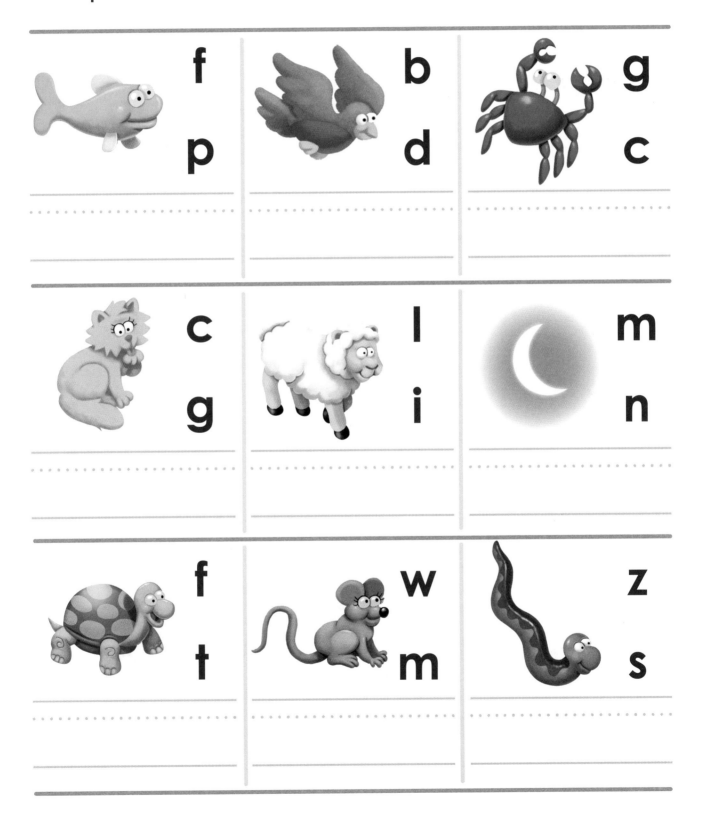

I Know the Sound

Say the name of the picture. Circle the letter that starts the picture name. Write the letter three times on the line.

I Know the Sound

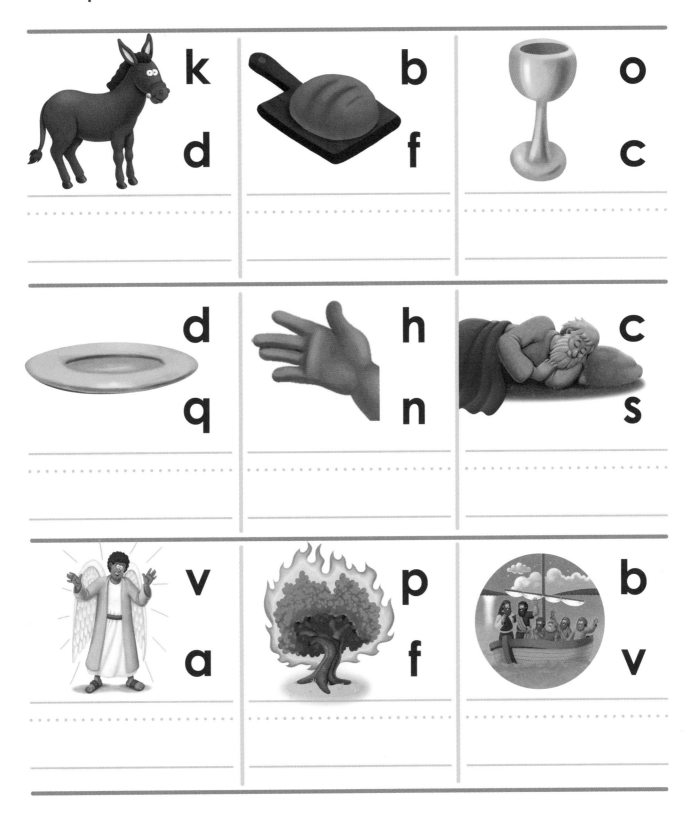

Say the name of the picture. Circle the letter that starts the picture name. Write the letter three times on the line.

k
d

b
f

o
c

d
q

h
n

c
s

v
a

p
f

b
v

You Are Paul

God changed Saul's name to Paul.
Circle PAUL.

SAUL

SAUL   PAUL

PAUL   PAUL

SAUL   SAUL

SAUL   PAUL

PAUL   SAUL

SAUL   SAUL

SAUL   PAUL

PAUL

Missing Letters

Something is missing! Write each missing letter.

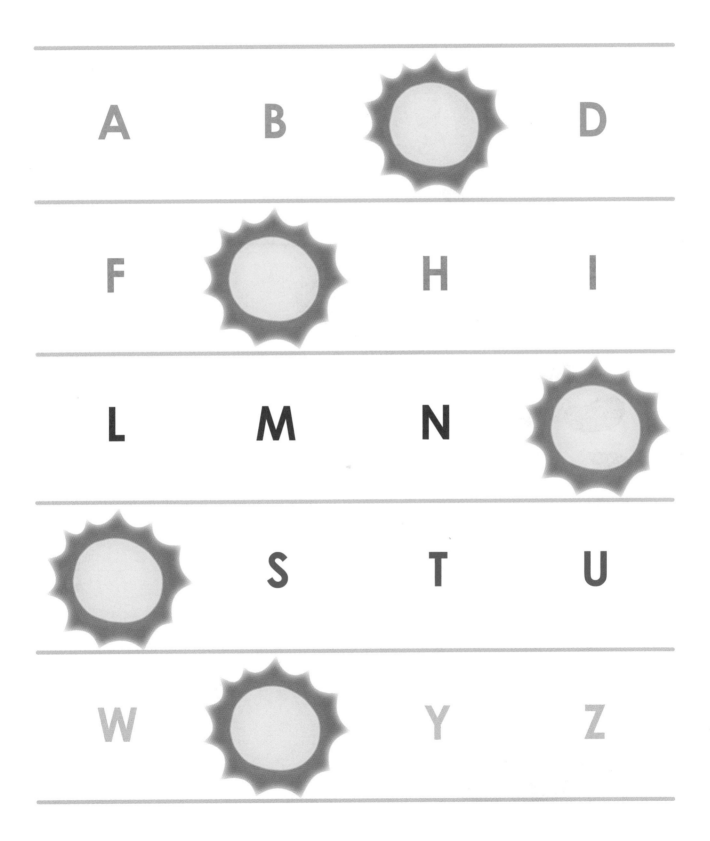

A   B   ☼   D

F   ☼   H   I

L   M   N   ☼

☼   S   T   U

W   ☼   Y   Z

How Does It Start

Match the letter to the picture with
the same beginning sound.

D

P

F

S

B

Letter Match-Up

Draw a line to match the uppercase
letter to its lowercase letter.

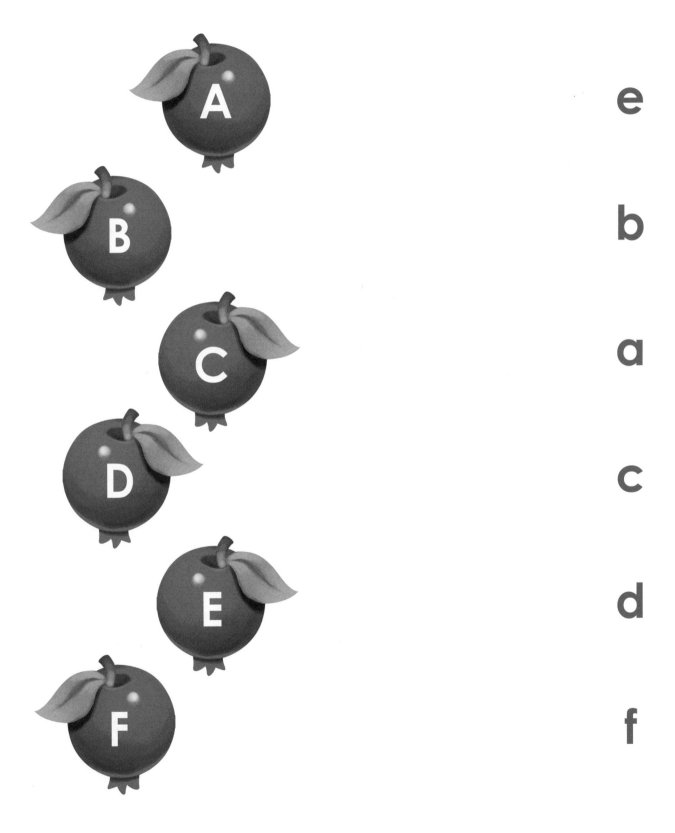

Letter Match-Up

Circle the matching lowercase letter.

M	n	h	m	w
N	p	n	s	v
O	o	c	a	k
P	g	b	t	p
Q	q	g	y	n
R	k	r	z	p

What Comes Next

Finish the alphabet. Write the missing letters in the bubbles.

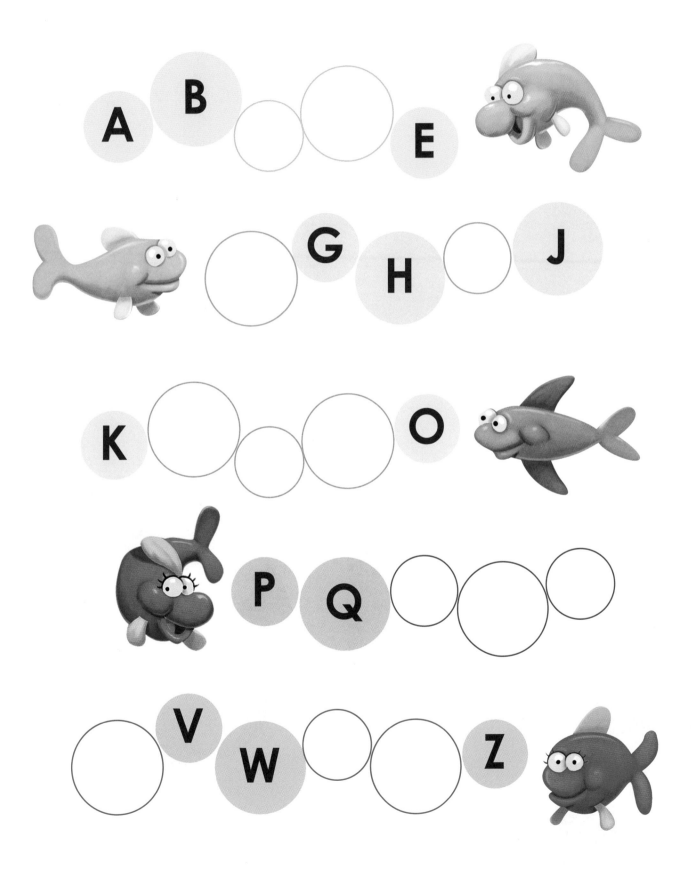

Learn the Number 1

Trace the number 1. Then write 1 on your own. Fill the lines.

There is 1 Jesus!
Circle baby Jesus.

1 dove

Learn the Word One

Trace the word one. Then write the word one. Fill the lines.

one

See lots of fish!
Circle 1 whale.

1 snake

Learn the Number 2

Trace the number 2. Then write 2 on your own. Fill the lines.

2 2 2

Noah's ark had 2 of every animal. Circle 2 lambs, 2 cats, and 2 giraffes.

2 butterflies

Learn the Word Two

Trace the word two. Then write the word two. Fill the lines.

two

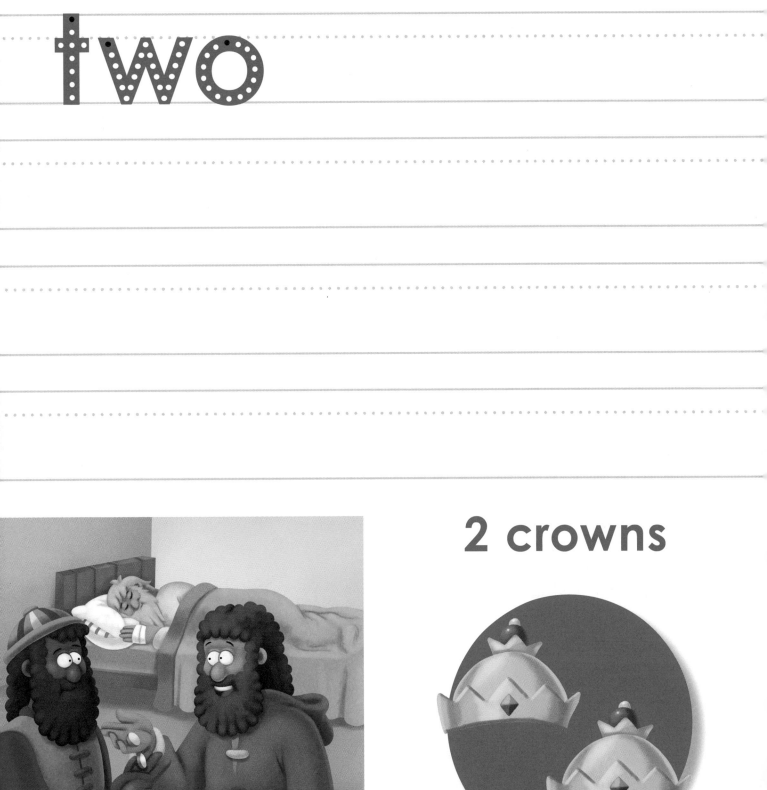

2 crowns

Can you count how many silver coins the man gave the innkeeper?

Learn the Number 3

Trace the number 3. Then write 3 on your own. Fill the lines.

333

Count the lions.
Now count the people.
Is the number the same?

3 arrows

Learn the Word Three

Trace the word three. Then write the word three. Fill the lines.

three

3 wise men

How many pigs
do you see?

Learn the Number 4

Trace the number 4. Then write 4 on your own. Fill the lines.

4 sheep

How many people are praying?

Learn the Word Four

Trace the word four. Then write the word four. Fill the lines.

four

4 soldiers

How many lizards are there?
How many feet does
each lizard have?

Learn the Number 5

Trace the number 5. Then write 5 on your own. Fill the lines.

Can you circle 5 clouds?

5 apples

Learn the Word Five

Trace the word five. Then write the word five. Fill the lines.

five

5 birds

Uh-oh, it's starting to rain!
Draw 5 raindrops.

Learn the Number 6

Trace the number 6. Then write 6 on your own. Fill the lines.

6 angels

**There are 6 trees.
Can you circle them all?**

Learn the Word Six

Trace the word six. Then write the word six. Fill the lines.

six

Draw a line connecting the birds. Count them as you go.

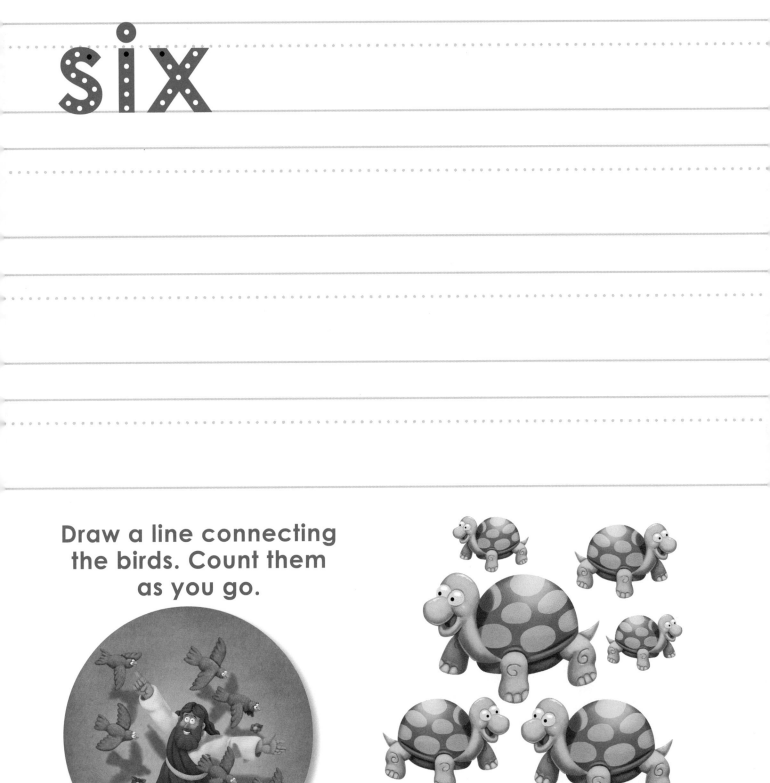

6 turtles

Learn the Number 7

Trace the number 7. Then write 7 on your own. Fill the lines.

7 fish

There are 4 red flowers and 3 blue flowers. How many are there all together?

Learn the Word Seven

Trace the word seven. Then write the word seven. Fill the lines.

seven

How many animals does Adam have?

7 jars

Learn the Number 8

Trace the number 8. Then write 8 on your own. Fill the lines.

8 children

Circle the bees in this picture.
How many are there?

Learn the Word Eight

Trace the word eight. Then write the word eight. Fill the lines.

eight

God gave the octopus eight
tentacles. Count them all.

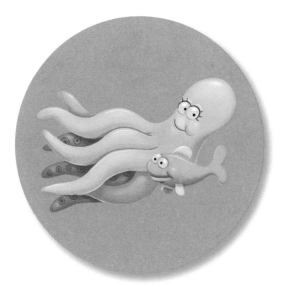

8
bags

Learn the Number 9

Trace the number 9. Then write 9 on your own. Fill the lines.

999

Can you circle all the butterflies? Count them. How many are there?

Jesus is the light of the world! Draw a flame on each lamp to match the center lamp. How many lamps are there?

Learn the Word Nine

Trace the word nine. Then write the word nine. Fill the lines.

nine

Can you circle 9 rabbits?

9 cups

Learn the Number 10

Trace the number 10. Then write 10 on your own. Fill the lines.

How many fish does
the fisherman have?

**Can you count how many sick
men there are?**

Learn the Word Ten

Trace the word ten. Then write the word ten. Fill the lines.

ten

Can you find 10 ears of corn?

There are 10 cats in this picture. Circle them.

Learn the Number 11

Trace the number 11. Then write 11 on your own. Fill the lines.

Find 11 sets of spooky eyes.

11 flies

Learn the Word Eleven

Trace the word eleven. Then write the word eleven. Fill the lines.

eleven

How many naughty frogs are there?

Can you count and circle 11 flying birds?

Learn the Number 12

Trace the number 12. Then write 12 on your own. Fill the lines.

How many people are listening to Jesus?

How many wheat bundles are in Joseph's dream?

Learn the Word Twelve

Trace the word twelve. Then write the word twelve. Fill the lines.

twelve

12 moons

Can you circle all the dogs?
How many are there?

The Number 1

Write the word one.

one

Draw one sun.

Match the number to
the groups with 1.

The Number 2

Write the word two.

two

Draw two stars.

Match the number to
the groups with 2.

2

The Number 3

Write the word three.

three

Draw three trees.

Match the number to
the groups with 3.

3

The Number 4

Write the word four.

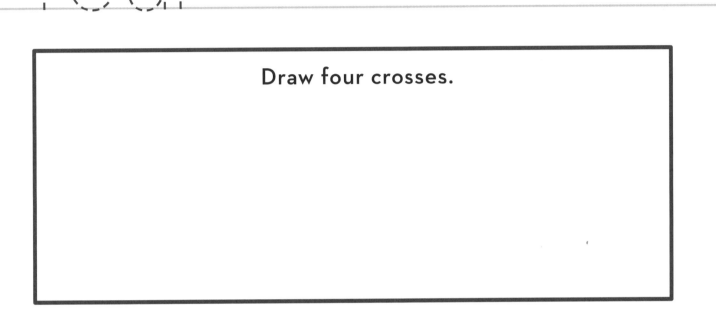

Draw four crosses.

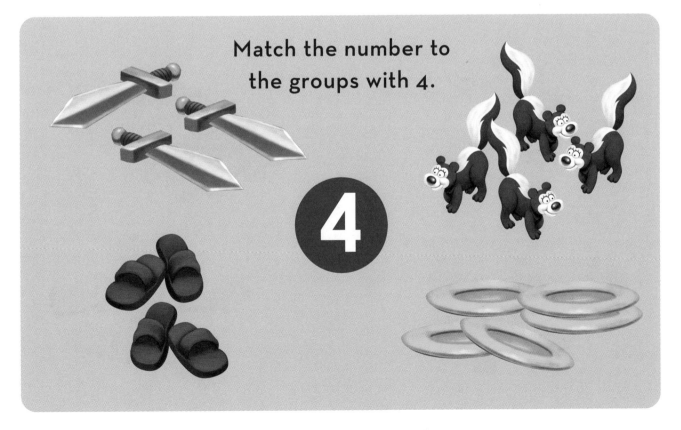

Match the number to
the groups with 4.

4

The Number 5

Write the word five.

five

Draw five people.

Match the number to the groups with 5.

5

BETHLEHEM

The Number 6

Write the word six.

six

Draw six apples.

Match the number to
the groups with 6.

The Number 7

Write the word seven.

seven

Draw seven hearts.

Match the number to the groups with 7.

7

The Number 8

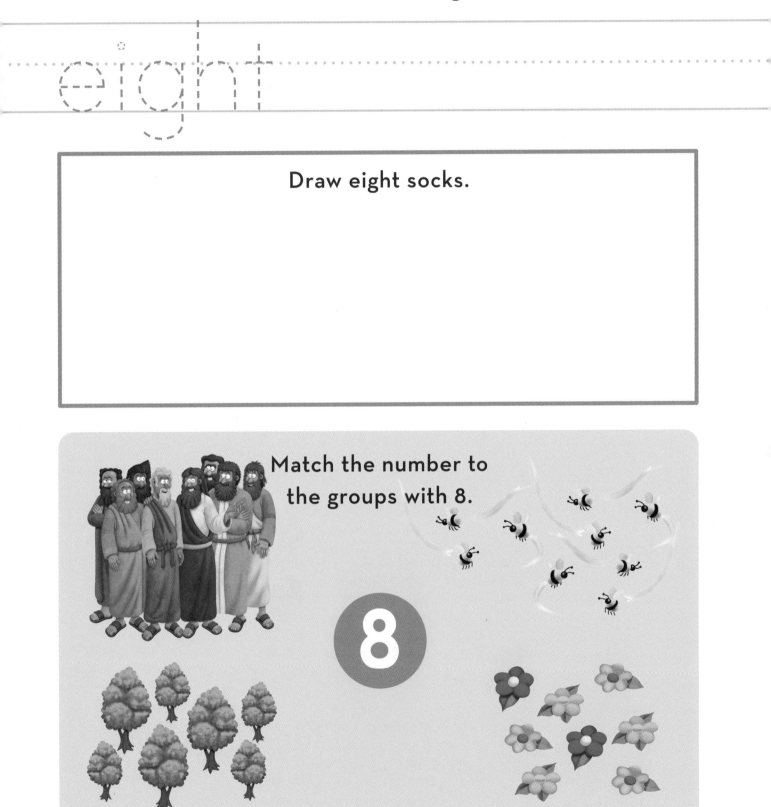

Write the word eight.

eight

Draw eight socks.

Match the number to the groups with 8.

8

The Number 9

Write the word nine.

nine

Draw nine balloons.

Match the number to
the group with 9.

9

The Number 10

Write the word ten.

ten

Draw ten clouds.

Match the number to
the group with 10.

10

The Number 11

Write the word eleven.

eleven

Draw eleven snowmen.

Match the number to the group with 11.

11

The Number 12

Write the word twelve.

twelve

Draw twelve cars.

Match the number to the group with 12.

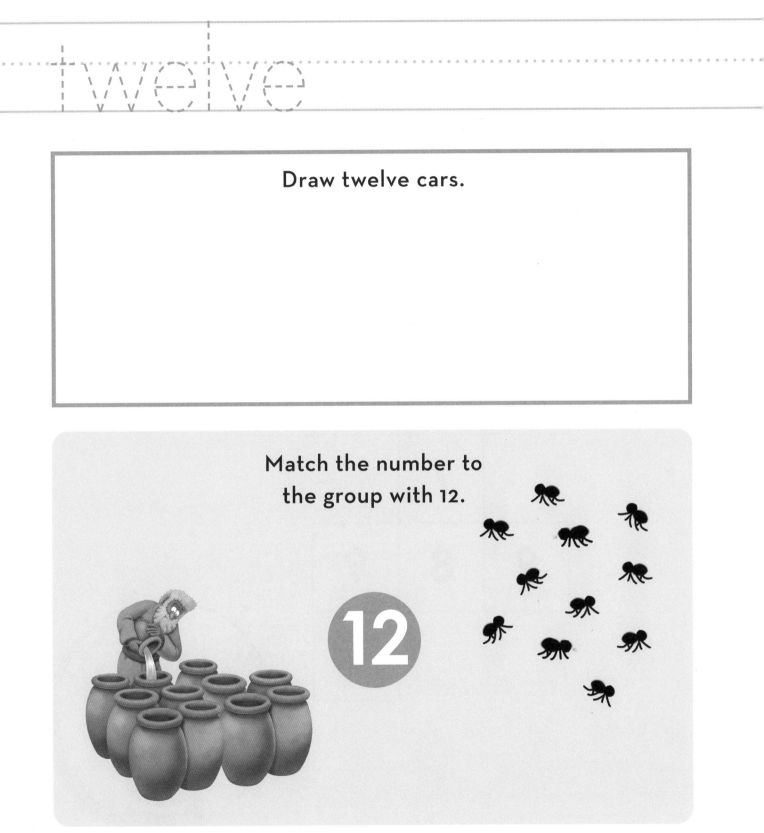

12

10 to 1

Only one man went back to thank Jesus. Follow the path from 1 to 10 forward, and then backward, to bring the man back to Jesus.

Match It Up

Draw a line matching the number to the group. One is done for you.

1

2

3

4

5

6

7

Count It Out

How many are on the page? Circle the number.

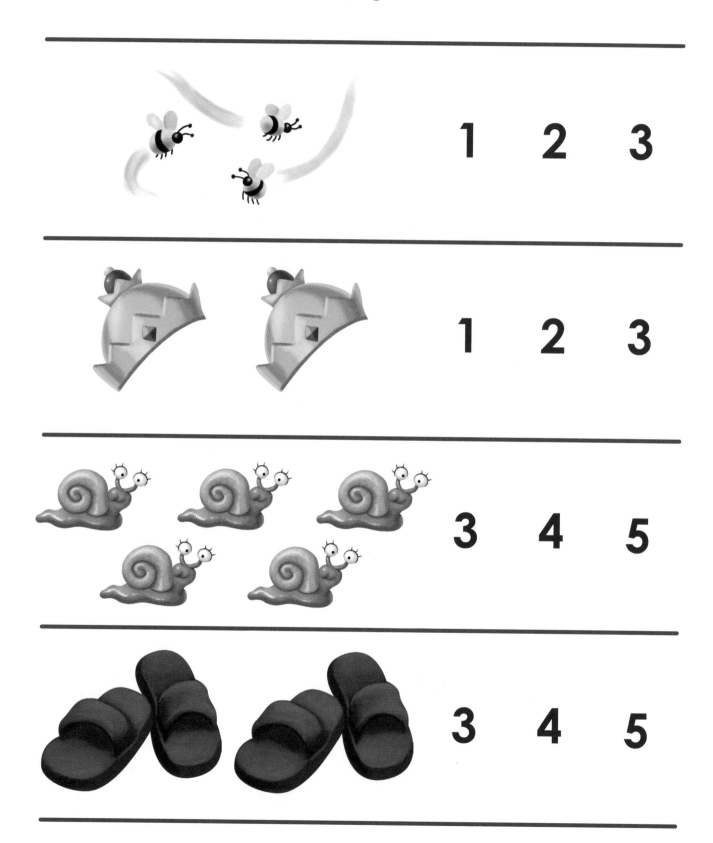

1 2 3

1 2 3

3 4 5

3 4 5

Missing Number

A shepherd watches over his sheep. He counts them.
Look at each row. Which number is missing?
Circle the missing number.

1	2		4	5 3 7

| 3 | | 5 | 6 | 2 3 4 |

| 4 | 5 | 6 | | 5 7 3 |

| 7 | | 9 | 10 | 8 6 4 |

Coins for the King

Zacchaeus collected tax money for the king. Count
Zacchaeus' coins. Trace the number of coins.

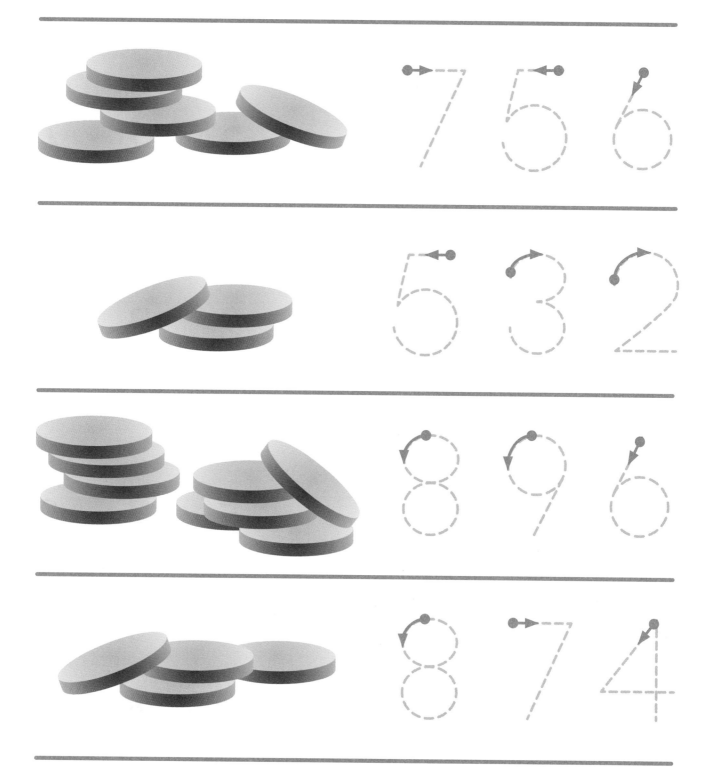

More Money

Zacchaeus promised Jesus he would give back all
the extra money he took. Trace the number. Circle
the coins that are MORE than the number.

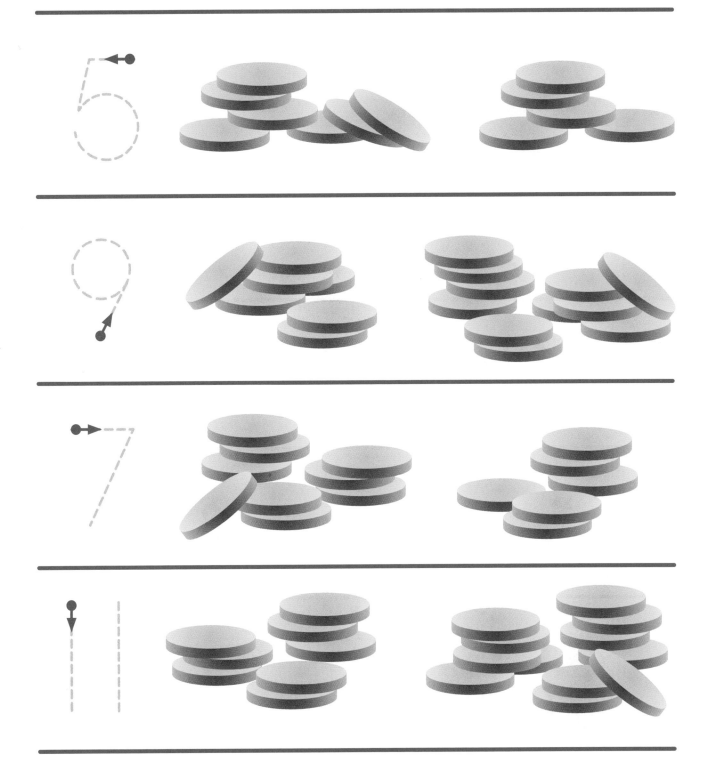

Count Them All

God asked Moses to help his people leave Egypt. Moses helped!
Count how many in each line.

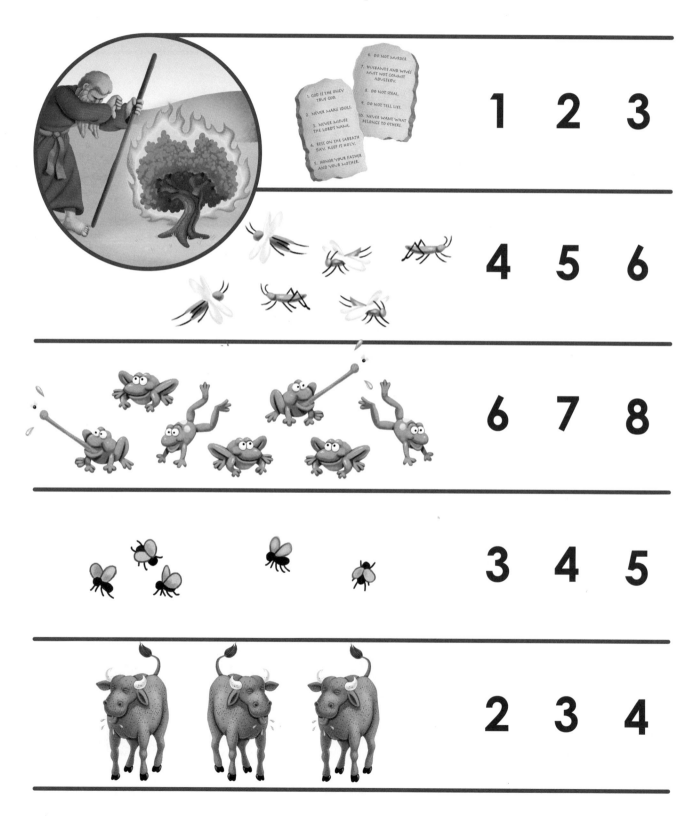

Count It Out

Look at God's creatures. Count each group
of creatures. Circle how many.

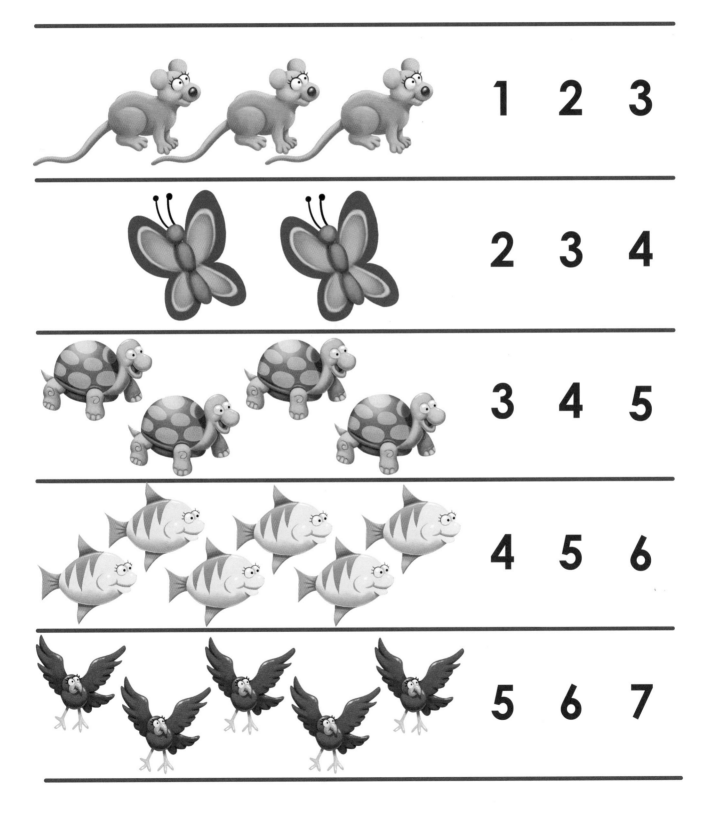

1 2 3

2 3 4

3 4 5

4 5 6

5 6 7

Jesus in a Garden

Jesus went to a special garden to pray. His disciples came too. Color the picture of Jesus.

Count how many stars: _____

Count how many flowers: _____

Missing Numbers

God made everything, even the clouds. Write
each missing number in the clouds.

1   2   4

2   3   4

6   8   9

   9   10   11

5   6   7

Everything Counts

God knows how many there are of everything.
Count and match the numbers with the items.

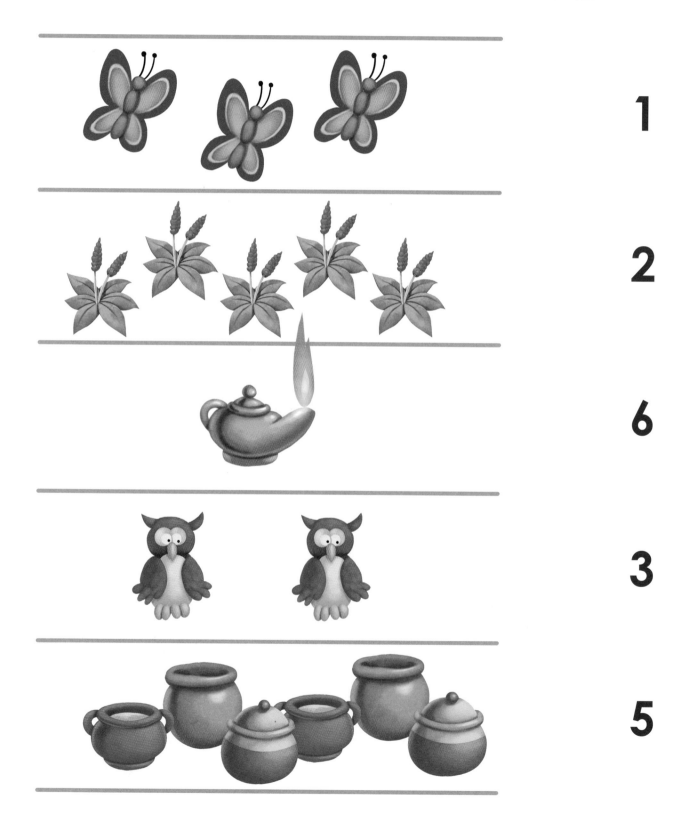

1

2

6

3

5

How Many Bees?

John the Baptist ate honey. Count the bees. Write how many in the box.

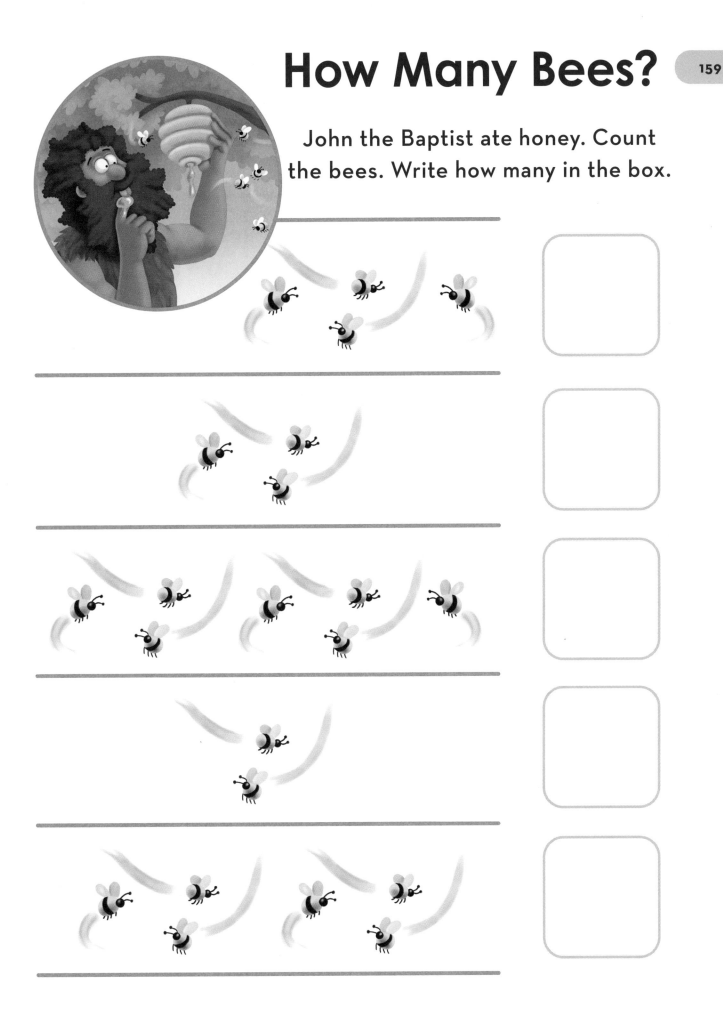

How Many Butterflies?

Count the butterflies. Circle the number.

1 3 4

0 5 1

5 6 7

9 10 6

4 5 3

7 8 5

1 2 3

8 7 9

6 7 4

How Many Fish?

Count the fish. Circle the number.

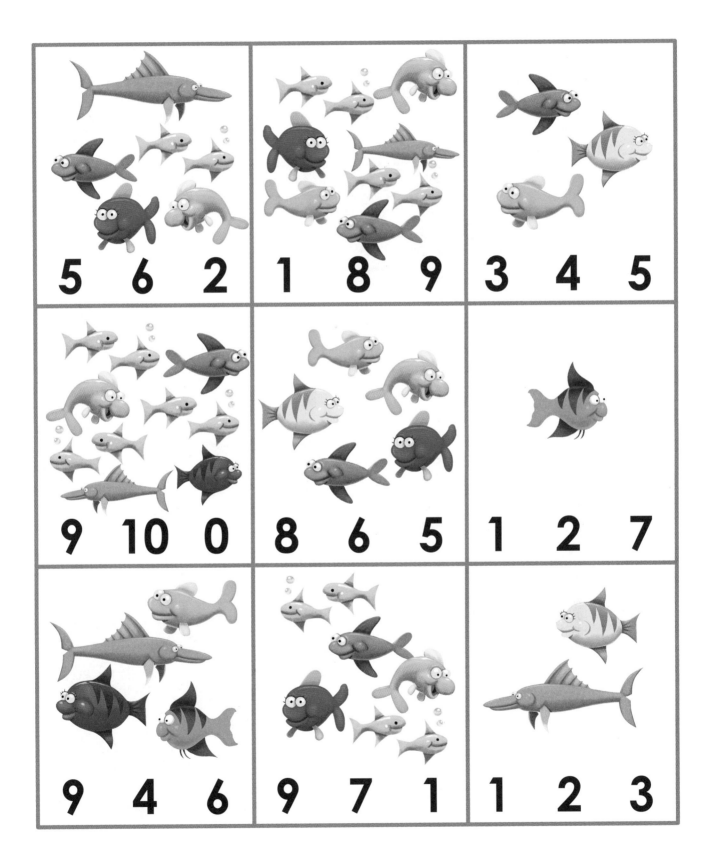

Where Is Eve?

Help Adam find Eve.

Where Is the Ark?

The dove found land. Help the dove find its way back to the ark.

Where To, Samuel?

Hannah brought Samuel to live at the tabernacle.
Lead Samuel to his bed in the tabernacle.

Let's Go, Mary and Joseph

Mary and Joseph need a place to stay.
Take the path to the stable.

The Lost Sheep

The shepherd looks everywhere for the lost sheep. He does not give up. Help the shepherd find his sheep.

Go Tell Them

Jesus rose on Easter Sunday. Help spread the news to his friends. Follow the path from the garden to his hiding friends.

A-Maze-Ing Power

Jesus healed lots of people who were sick. Help the men bring their sick friend to see Jesus.

Ruth and Naomi

Naomi's husband died. She wanted to go back to her home in Israel. Her daughter-in-law Ruth went with her. Help Naomi and Ruth find Israel.

Baby in a Basket

Help baby Moses float safely in the
maze to Pharaoh's daughter.

Adam Loves Animals

Adam loved all the animals God made. Follow the path.
Help Adam find the elephant, monkey, and lion!

On the Way to Bethlehem

The king wanted to count all the people in the kingdom. Mary and Joseph went to Bethlehem. Help them find their way to Bethlehem in the maze.

Which Is Bigger?

Circle the picture that is bigger than the first one.

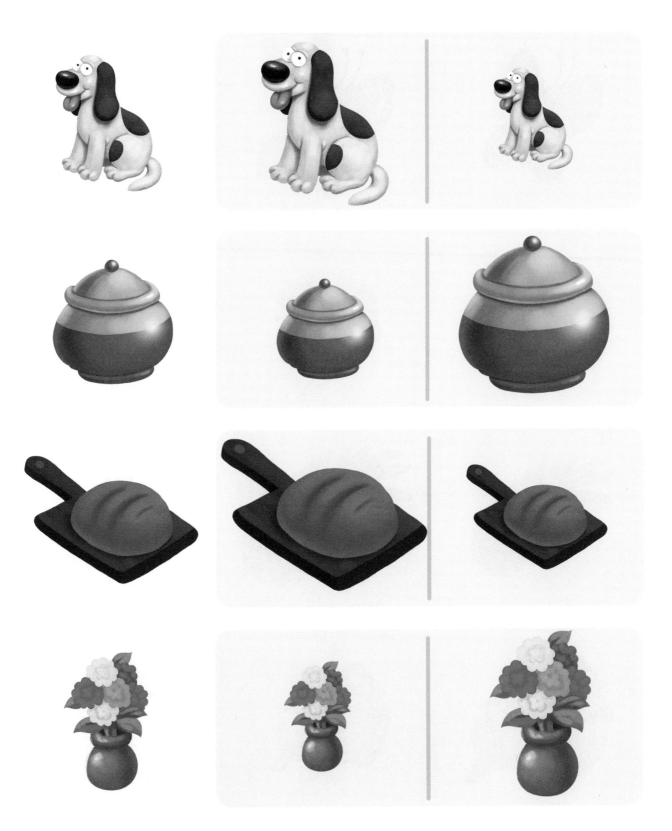

Which Is Smaller?

Circle the picture that is smaller than the first one.

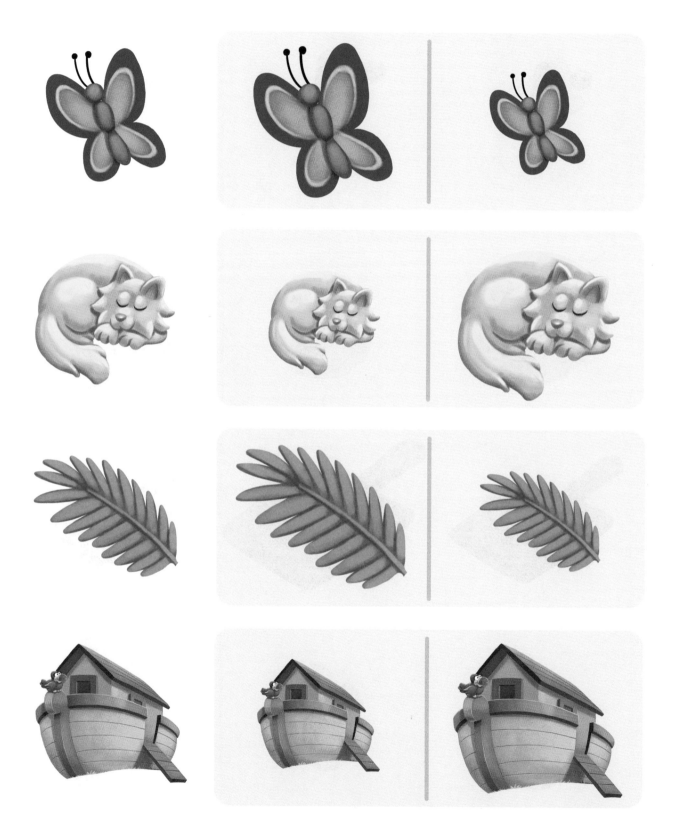

The Same

Circle 2 that are the same in each row.

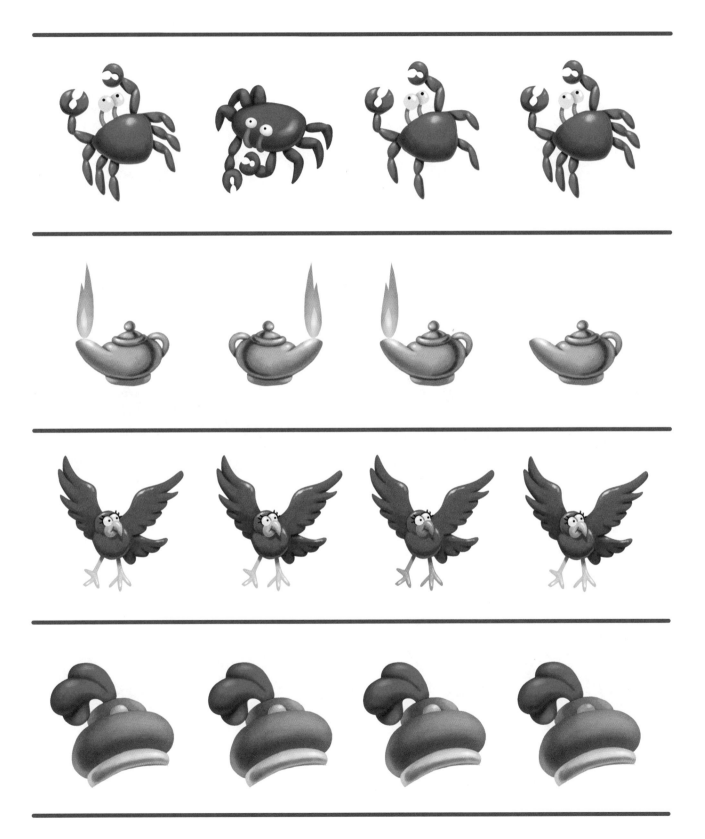

Matching

Circle the 2 that are exactly the same.

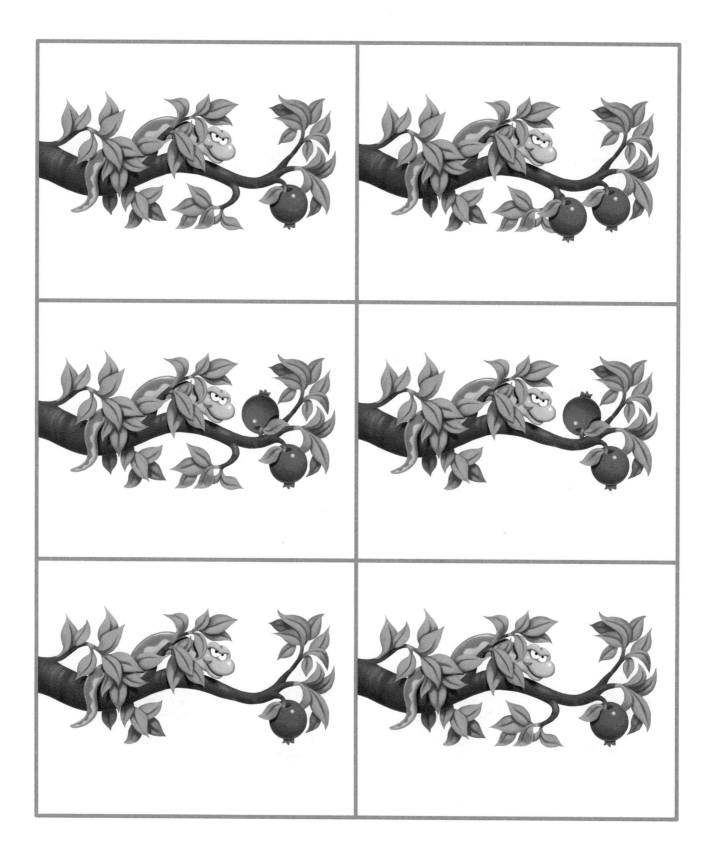

Being Different Is OK

King Solomon wants to know the difference.
Circle the picture that is different.

All the Same

The angels said, "Jesus will return the
same way you saw him go."
Color the picture that is the same as the first one.

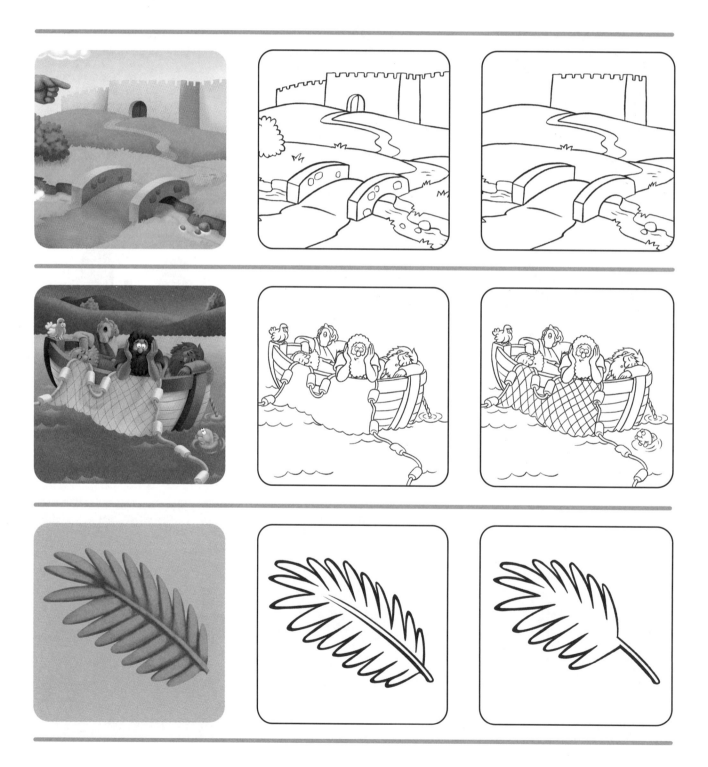

Daniel and the Lions' Den

King Darius made a new law. For 30 days, everyone had to pray only to him. Daniel knew that was wrong. He still prayed to God! Look at the pictures below. Circle the 6 differences.

With God's Help

The Bible is filled with heroes. These are people who listened to God. Some of the heroes were small but they did big things. Look at each pair. Circle what is bigger.

What's the Difference?

God made all the creature of the world. He made a man named Adam. Look at the two pictures. Circle the 5 differences.

Then trace Adam's name.

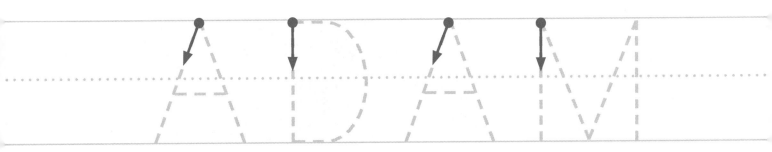

Not the Son?

Jesus said he was the Son of God. That made the men angry. Look at the pictures. Find 5 differences. Circle the differences.

The Savior Is Born!

Baby Jesus was born in a stable. Mary wrapped him in strips of cloth. She laid him in a manger. Look at the two pictures. Can you find 5 different things? Circle them.

Which One Is Different?

We are all special. Circle the picture that is different.

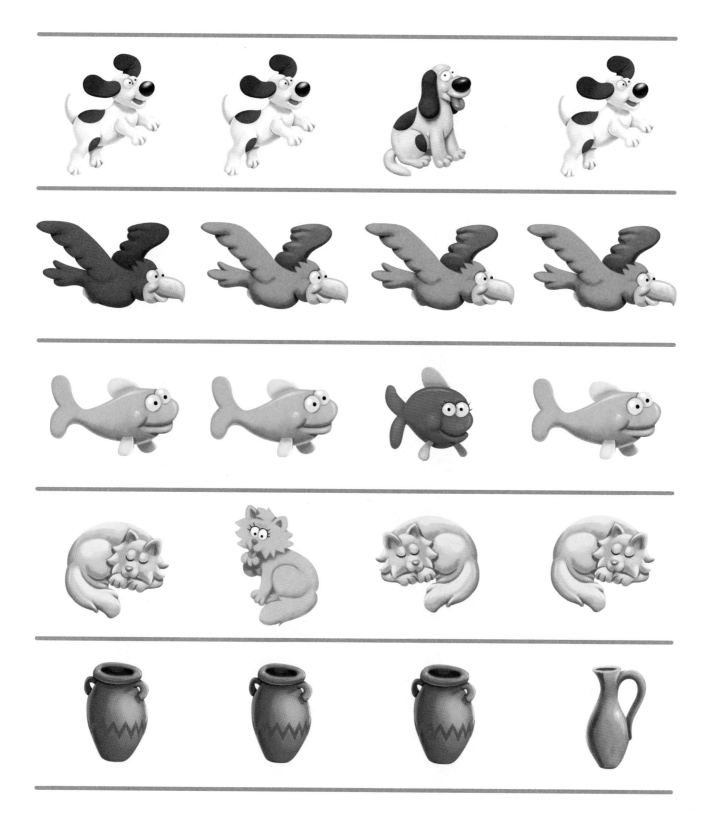

I See a Difference

God makes us all different. Circle the picture that is different.

All Things Big and Small

God makes big things and small things. Circle the smallest.

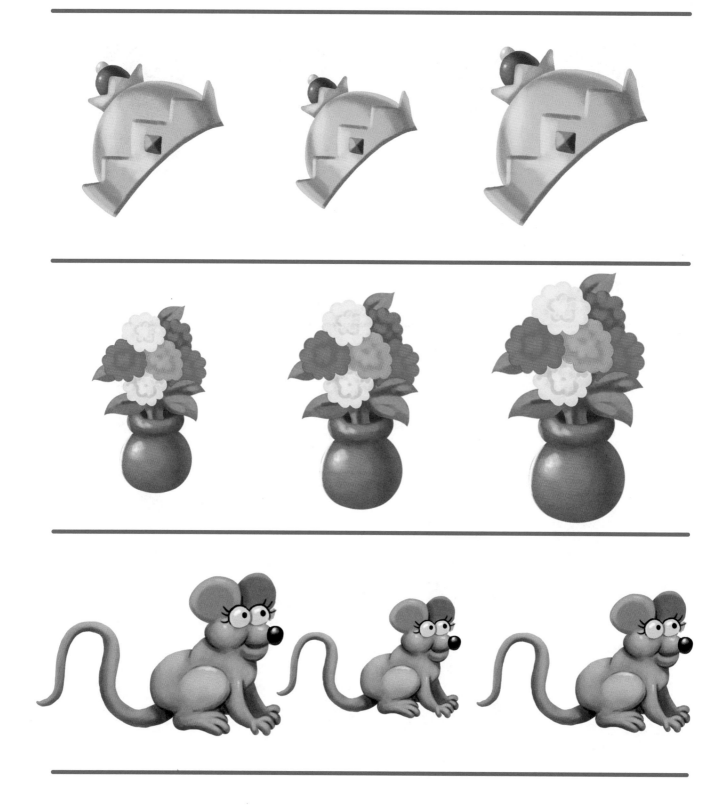

All Things Small and Big

God makes small things and big things. Circle the biggest.

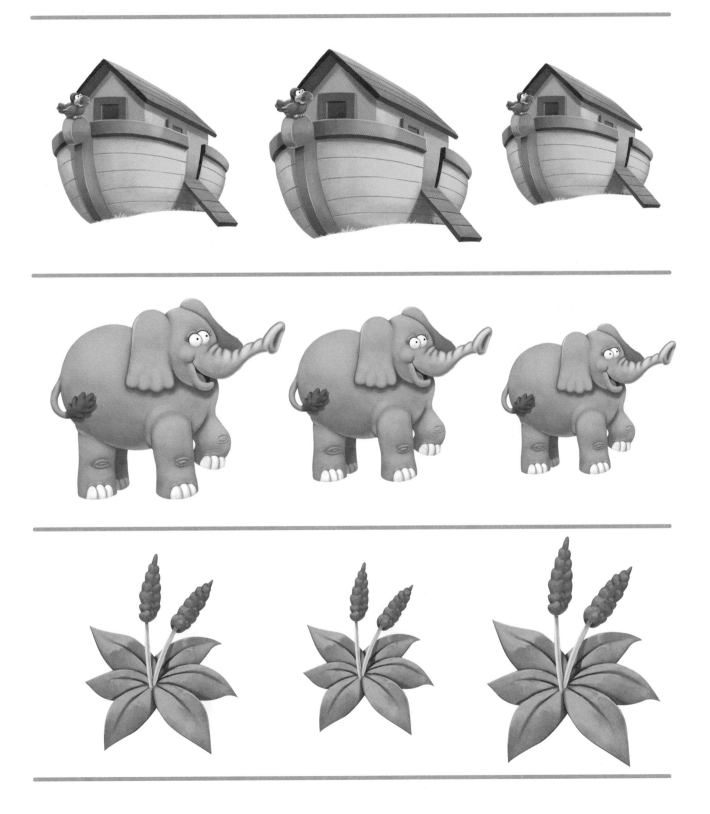

All Things Tall and Short

God makes tall things and short things. Circle the tallest.

All Things Short and Tall

God makes short and tall things. Circle the shortest.

Noah Loved God

Noah loved God.
Circle the picture that completes the pattern.

A Pattern of Giving

Jesus said the widow gave from her heart.
Draw the shape that comes next.

What Is Next?

Circle the one that comes next.

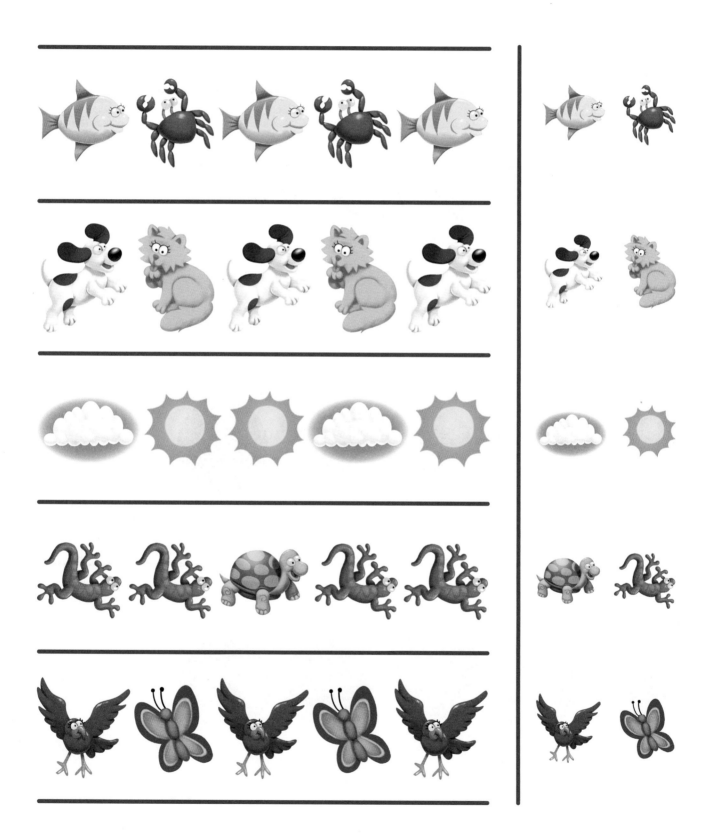

And Jesus Grew!

Baby Jesus grew up and became a kid just like you! Color in the picture. Use the chart to help you pick colors.

1=blue 2=red 3=brown 4=yellow 5=orange 6=purple

A Beautiful World

God created everything! Connect the dots to
finish the picture. Color the picture.

The Third Day

Jesus died. But three days later an angel came to the tomb! He said, "Jesus is not here!" Connect the dots around the angel. Count to 12.

A Sign From God

Three Wise Men were looking for baby Jesus. God gave them a sign to help them find the baby. What was the sign? Connect the dots 1–10 to see the sign God gave the Wise Men on their way to see Jesus.

The First Miracle

Jesus's first miracle was at a wedding feast. Look at the picture below. Circle the 6 things that do not belong at a wedding party.

Jesus Loves Children

Jesus loved to have children around him.

Look at the picture. Find the 12 squirrels. Circle them.

Hannah's Prayer

Hannah loved God. She wanted to have a baby to love. Hannah prayed to God. Match the mother animals with their babies. Draw a line.

Match the Words

Match the picture with the word. Draw a line.

cup

bug

dog

cat

What's My Name?

Match the picture with the word. Draw a line.

bee

sun

tree

fish

I Can Write My Name

I Can Write My Name

Practice Sheet

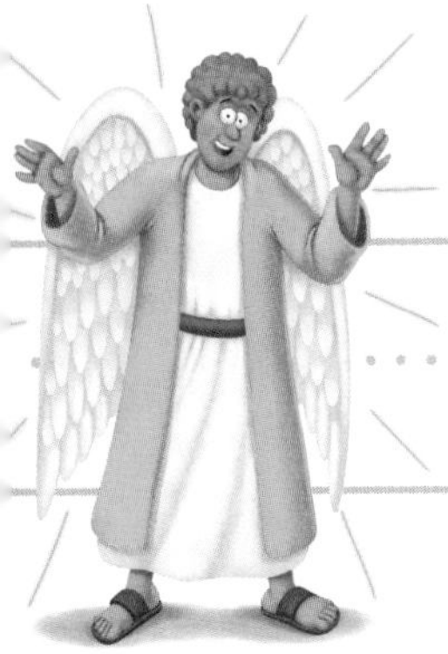

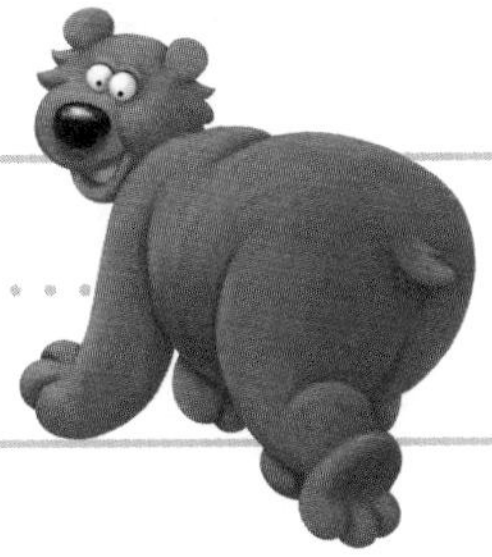

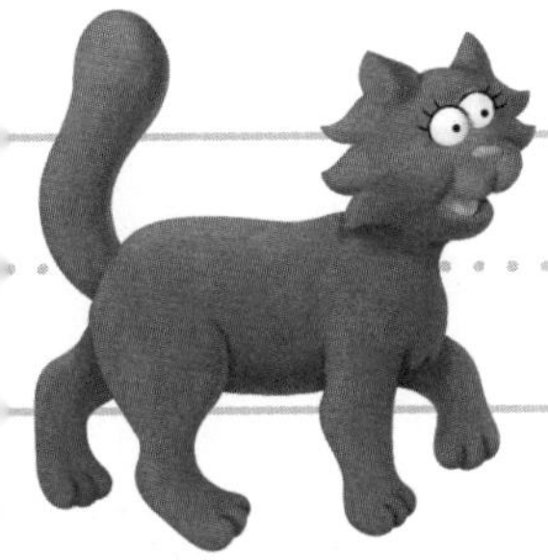

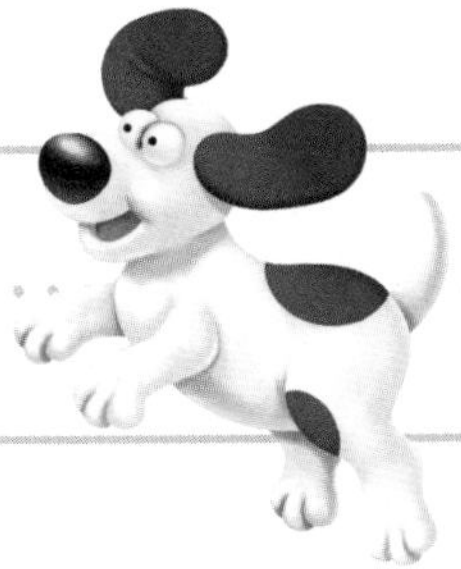

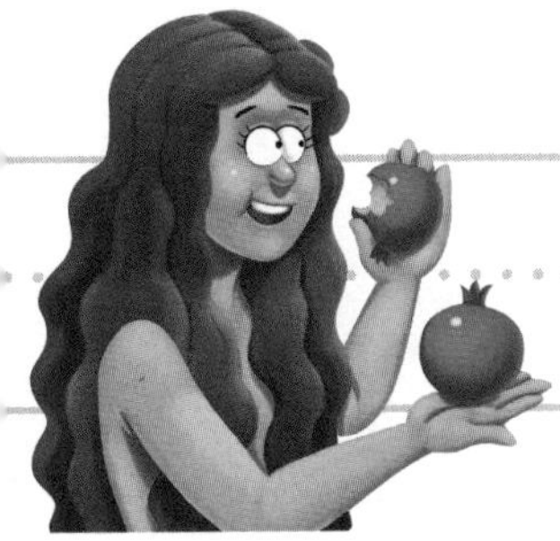

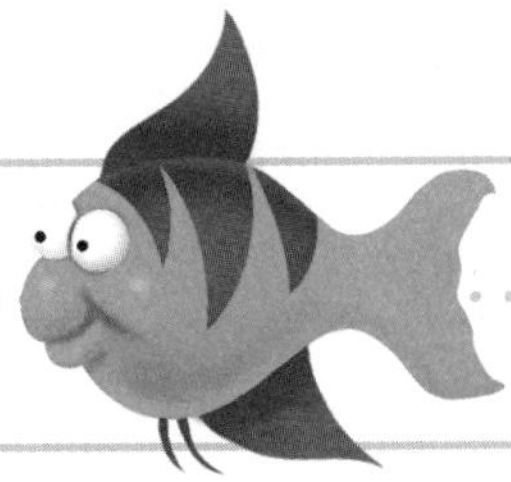

Practice Sheet

Practice Sheet

Building foundations of faith with children for over 30 years!

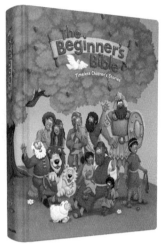

9780310750130
$16.99 / Hardcover

The Beginner's Bible® has been a favorite with young children and their parents since its release in 1989 with over 25 million products sold. While several updates have been made since its early days, *The Beginner's Bible®* will continue to build a foundation of faith in little ones for many more years to come.

Full of faith and fun, *The Beginner's Bible®* is a wonderful gift for any child. The easy-to-read text and bright, full-color illustrations on every page make it a perfect way to introduce young children to the stories and characters of the Bible. With new vibrant three-dimensional art and compelling text, more than 90 Bible stories come to life. Kids ages 6 and under will enjoy the fun illustrations of Noah helping the elephant onto the ark, Jonah praying inside the fish, and more, as they discover *The Beginner's Bible®* just like millions of children before. *The Beginner's Bible®* was named the 2006 Retailers Choice Award winner in Children's Nonfiction.

More products from *The Beginner's Bible®* to discover:

The Beginner's Bible
Little Lamb's Christmas
9780310770589

The Beginner's Bible
First 100 Bible Words
9780310766858

The Beginner's Bible
Learn Your Letters
9780310770244

The Beginner's Bible
All Aboard Noah's Ark
9780310768678

The Beginner's Bible
Super Girls of the Bible
Sticker and Activity Book
9780310751182

The Beginner's Bible
All About Jesus Sticker
and Activity Book
9780310746935

The Beginner's Bible
I Can Read Jonah and
the Giant Fish
9780310743286

The Beginner's Bible
People of the Bible
9780310765035